PLANNING YOUR PREACHING

J. Winston Pearce

BROADMAN PRESS
Nashville, Tennessee

Dewey Decimal Classification Number: 251
Library of Congress Catalog Card Number: 67–19398
Printed in the United States of America

Preface

The purpose of this book is clearly stated in the title, *Planning Your Preaching*. The aim is to define what is meant by the phrase "planning your preaching," to persuade the reader of the need for performing the task, and to give suggestions as to how the job may be done.

The book grows out of twenty-five years in the pastoral ministry and out of considerably less time in the teaching ministry. In the pastoral ministry I learned the absolute necessity for long-range planning of a preaching program if there was to be any semblance of order, effectiveness, and wholeness to the proclamation of the gospel. In the classroom I have seen how eagerly the alert ministerial student grasps for help in this area, and I have witnessed the gratitude of those same students when they have followed the plan in their pastorates.

My indebtedness to others is overwhelming: competent authors, understanding congregations, diligent students, effective pastors have all made their contributions to the author and to the book. Grateful acknowledgment has been made wherever it was possible to do so.

It is my hope that the book may prove helpful to teachers of preaching and to pastors of churches. They both know the pertinence of the lesson that Aesop's grasshopper learned from the ant: "It is thrifty to prepare today for the wants of tomorrow."

To that loyal band of men and women
    in four pastorates:
    The First Baptist Church of Nevada, Missouri
    The First Baptist Church of Durham, North Carolina
    The Seventh Baptist Church of Baltimore, Maryland
    The First Baptist Church of De Land, Florida
who through encouragement, understanding, and wise church-
manship made it possible for me to plan preaching programs

Contents

1

The Plan Is the Thing

It is one thing to be ready to preach; it is a different thing to be prepared to preach. It is necessary that a man be ready and willing. We warm to the preacher who says, "Woe is me if I preach not the gospel," who feels that the Word of God is as a fire in his bones. Nothing takes the place of conviction and passion in a preacher.

But, effective preaching requires more. It requires preparedness. Ahimaaz was ready to carry the news of battle to his king; he was not prepared to bear the news of the battle.

The preacher must be both ready and prepared. No amount of preparation will suffice for a deficiency in passion. Proof of this is not hard to find. Many of the best qualified preachers from the standpoint of formal education, attested to by respected degrees from reputable seminaries and divinity schools, are sadly lacking in effectiveness as preachers. And, many a hot-hearted, emotion-charged illiterate man without worthy preparation finds himself in the same situation. Both fire and light are essential—fire at the heart and light at the head.

On being asked to define the word deacon, the boy replied, "A deacon is something you set fire to and put on a hill." No, that is a "beacon." But it is not a bad definition of what both preachers and deacons should be—those who stand on a hill with light and heat.

The Need for a Plan

It is difficult to see how any "ready" preacher can be a "prepared" preacher without careful, long-range planning. It is not claimed

1

that if a man plans his year's preaching program in the summer, his people will thereby, ipso facto, be guaranteed good sermons throughout the year. Much work is required between the hours of planning and the hours of preaching.

The need for a planned preaching program is especially apparent among the freer of the free Protestant churches. The reason is easy to see. Often there is no guidance for these ministers in their preaching programs. This is not true for the Roman Catholic, the Orthodox, nor for the more liturgical denominations among the Protestants. These have their plans and schedules, some of which are better than others. But even the best of plans can be abused, and no one of the plans guarantees a successful preaching program.

There is a desperate need for all ministers to have some guidance in what they will preach to their people from week to week and from year to year. The pastor should be able to say to his people what Jeremiah heard God saying to the exiles: "I know the plans I have for you . . . plans for welfare and not for evil, to give you a future and a hope" (29:11, RSV).

For the preacher to have no plan is to leave him to follow his own inclinations. His inclinations—in many cases the harsher word "prejudices" might be used—may be based upon many things: early or late influences, limited instruction, the whims of his people, current theological winds, a desire to reach a particular type of person in the community, the immediate promotional emphasis from denominational headquarters, some recently read book, or a magazine article clipped from *Reader's Digest*. Each of these areas may be effectively and helpfully used if made to heel to some worthy, long-range plan, but no one of the above should be followed without an overall plan.

Types of Plans

The plan that a preacher uses must be his own. In James Street's novel *Good-bye, My Lady*, the storekeeper comes to tell Uncle Jesse that the owners of his grandson's dog have been found. The problem is whether they should tell Skeeter or let him keep the dog. Cash says, "It's your load." Uncle Jesse responds, "I'll tote it."

Every preacher has his own load in the form of a decision about preaching plans, and he has to tote that responsibility. No one can tote it for him. If he chooses to use a plan, what will that plan be, how much of it will he use, and how closely will he stick to it? Each preacher must tote his own load.

This book deals with different plans by which a man may organize his preaching. These methods will be explained in detail as they are discussed. There will, of necessity, be some overlapping and repetition in the discussion of the different plans. There is no way to avoid this. There is not a different gospel for each plan. There is but one gospel. The different plans must be made to serve the one gospel, or the plans have no reason for being. Too, there are great days like Christmas and Easter to be observed in every plan. Further, the discussion of each plan needs to be complete within itself so that the reader will not have to turn back to plans already discussed for the complete pattern being recommended.

The unit of time suggested here for planning is a twelve-month period. It may be that a preacher should think in terms of a five-year period for major themes or for the overall sweep of the Scriptures that he will use in his preaching. Certainly, every man should give careful consideration to the preaching he has done in former years when he comes to plan his preaching for the year ahead.

Still, all things considered, the best unit of time for planning a preaching program is the twelve-month period. Since this is the calendar year, it is the unit of time that is most often used in other forms of planning.

The twelve-month period gives enough time for a man to observe the content of his preaching objectively, yet is brief enough for a man to change his plan if he feels that it is not serving his people's needs effectively nor bringing the greatest glory to his God.

A warning to the preacher: One must not *over*plan. A preaching plan is often like the plan for a city, park, playground, or home: some of its best features are the result of accidents! Another caution: It is a bad plan that admits of no modification. A wise preaching program not only provides for a reasonable amount of planning, but it also allows a good deal of flexibility. A wise teacher will not go before her class without a teaching plan, nor will her plan be overly rigid. That would be as bad as having no plan. Whatever the lesson plan may be, the wise teacher will be ready and able to adapt it to take advantage of classroom conditions. When she has her lesson plan well in mind, she can encourage her students to take brief excursions along the way. The learning experience is more interesting and valuable for these side trips. Still, the good teacher can always lead her students back to the main trail of subject matter, which points toward her purposeful goal.

Preparing the Plan

When and where does a pastor plan his preaching program? Again, every man has his own load and must tote it for himself. The time and the place that are essential for one man cannot be found by another; and, if such time and place could be found, they could not be used effectively.

However, many find that they can accomplish most in an isolated atmosphere during the enforced leisure of a vacation period. The amount of time you as a minister are allowed for your vacation should depend, among other things, on how much time you can effectively use. Vacations are not just for rest; they are primarily for work—the kind of work that you cannot effectively do under the pressure of your normal pastoral duties. G. K. Chesterton once said that he could not understand people who could not successfully "do nothing."

There are some who complain of a man for doing nothing; there are some, still more mysterious and amazing, who complain of having nothing to do. When actually presented with some beautiful blank hours or days, they will grumble at their blankness. When given the gift of loneliness, which is the gift of liberty, they will cast it away; they will destroy it deliberately with some dreadful game of cards or a little ball. I speak only for myself; I know it takes all sorts to make a world; but I cannot repress a shudder when I see them throwing away their hard won holidays by doing something. For my own part, I never can get enough Nothing to do. I feel as if I had never had leisure to unpack a tenth part of the luggage of my life and thoughts.[1]

That is not only good writing, it is good sense. Chesterton is not against work, he is against misspent leisure. That matter of finding leisure to unpack the luggage of one's life and thoughts points toward a creative vacation.

If a minister can find some relatively isolated spot—far enough from his church to keep his people from feeling that they can drive out to discuss matters with him, or that he can drive in for any celebration or difficulty that might arise—he has the makings of a good place to unpack the luggage of life and thought and get his planning done. If he will get to bed at a reasonable time in the evening, get up at an early hour in the morning, and put in five hours of good work each morning while the family sleeps, he can get his planning done without too much self-righteousness! Then he can join his family for the noon meals, spend the afternoons and evenings with his wife and children, and the day will be well spent.

If a minister is given a month's vacation (some churches give more, many give less), he should be able to spend six days each week for three out of the four weeks of his vacation in study. That will give him ninety hours for reading and planning. If he has collected a reasonable amount of material during the year and has made adequate notes on the assets and liabilities of his present preaching plan, ninety hours should be adequate. He will return from a profitable, creative, and enjoyed vacation. It will have been a vacation that brought him re-creation, as well as recreation.

The coming year will be brighter, every day of it, for the way the minister *invested* his vacation. There will be fewer hungry sheep who look up and remain hungry. The minister will have fewer sleepless nights. He will be less likely to develop ulcers, and his family will find him easier to live with. He just might find ways to spend more time with the family, and the family just might be glad to have him do it!

Edward Steichen, brother-in-law of Carl Sandburg and one of America's greatest photographers, traveled all over the world taking rare photographs. Many of these became famous. The time came, however, when due to age and health it was impossible for Steichen to travel. He then limited his picture-taking to just what he could photograph from the windows of his home. Over a period of three years, at different times during the days and nights, he took hundreds of pictures of a shadblow tree (a flowering shrub) across a pond from his bedroom window. Steichen never took more exquisite pictures! [2]

Obviously, it will not always be possible for a minister to have a month to spend in some secluded retreat. Some ministers will *never* be able to have such a vacation under such circumstances. It may be necessary to reserve one hour each morning in the regular schedule for a period of three months. It may be best to reserve one full morning each week, or one full day in the month, or one evening each week, for whatever length of time necessary to get the job done.

However, it can be done. A minister is not permitted the luxury of saying that he has neither the time nor the place needed to plan his preaching program. That is like sitting at a lunch counter saying you have nowhere to eat lunch; it is like saying that you are too sick to call a doctor, too hungry to eat, or too cold to get warm!

What are the ingredients of a planned preaching program? The answer depends upon the plan chosen. Any plan would probably require at least the following items: (1) the date; (2) the emphasis (emphasis in the Christian Year: Christmas, Easter, Pentecost, Palm Sunday; in the national calendar: Washington's birthday, Labor Day, Fourth of July; in the denominational calendar: missions, education, Layman's Day; in the local church calendar: the church's anniversary, Vacation Bible School, annual picnic); (3) the sermon subject; (4) the Scripture reference (the Scripture lessons, Old and New Testament, plus text), and (5) any leading idea relating to the development of the sermon.

The Mechanics of the Plan

A preaching chart is needed upon which to place the above information. The chart may be as large or as small, as elaborate or as simple as interest, taste, ability, and resources dictate. It can be as simple as twelve sheets of 8½ by 11 typewriter paper, each sheet to represent one month of the preaching plan. Mark off four vertical lines and five horizontal lines on each sheet. Allow one inch of free space at the top of the page for marking the designated month, and one-half inch at the left side for marking the designated week. There will be twenty squares, each two inches in diameter.

Moving from left to right across the page, write "Events" over the top of the first square; "A.M." over the second square; "P.M." over the third square; and "Wednesday" over the top of the last square. This gives space for listing the content of the three normal weekly services (Sunday morning, Sunday evening, and Wednesday evening) for a month.

In the first column for each week, list the events suggested for that Sunday and week in the Christian, civic, denominational[3] and local calendars—events that have some bearing upon the preaching program. The event may not be sufficiently important to require a full sermon; it may need only an illustration or reference in the sermon.

In the second and third squares, list the subject and, if possible, the title of the sermon, the Scripture lessons including the text, and any leading sermon idea that may occur to you at this time. In the last square, much the same approach can be made for the midweek services. A chapter will follow, suggesting opportunities and possibilities for this service. (An example of such a chart is given at the close of this chapter.)

When the twelve sheets have been worked out, one sheet for each of the twelve months in the year's preaching program, fasten the sheets together (*Scotch Magic Mending Tape* is good). Then attach them to a piece of heavy poster board, 28 by 44 inches.

The joined and completed chart needs to be accessible to the preacher at all times when he is in his study. It can be placed on the wall if there is adequate space adjacent to the desk, or it can be placed on a good, stout easel with plyboard base. The preferable place is the top of the desk, possibly under a glass top. If the desk top is not sufficiently large to accommodate so large a chart, two things can be done. First, he may be able to buy a desk with a larger top, which will be expensive. Or, he may purchase a large piece of good, half-inch plyboard from the lumber mill or cabinet shop. With a little nonprofessional surface conditioning and varnishing, the plywood makes a beautiful top, and the whole cost will probably be less than twenty dollars. With this arrangement the minister can have his year's preaching program always before him as he works at his desk.

Probably the most attractive feature of this type of preaching chart is that the single sheets, representing one month of the total plan, can be worked in a typewriter. For the average minister this means clarity and economy of space. However, the preaching plan may be written or lettered directly on the poster board. The entire year's program can be put on a single board, 28 by 44 inches.

Four smaller boards, one for each quarter of the year, can be used. One of these at a time may be kept on the desk, being replaced by the next quarterly chart as it is needed, and so on through the year. However, there is advantage in having the entire year's preaching program in sight at all times. In reading, in clipping ideas, in filing illustrations, in checking calendars, it will be needed. If the entire year's program is not in front of the minister, he will not use it as often as he needs to use it. He simply will not turn from his desk to a file, or get up from his desk to check through charts for the desired information.

The particular type of preaching chart that is chosen can be used for any preaching plan a minister uses. Whichever plan he uses, he will need to have the chart before him.

Once the preaching plan has been decided upon, the type of chart to be used chosen, and the material placed on the chart, it is time to get the material into a workable filing system. Again, regardless of the preaching plan and the preaching chart, the filing will need to be done, and the same filing arrangement can be used regardless of the plan and chart.

A work sheet roughly 11 by 17 inches (the exact size of two sheets of standard size typewriter paper joined side by side) can be made up by a printer in pads of one hundred sheets. The pads should have a medium-weight cardboard back to give stability.

The necessary guidelines and headings would be put in by the printer. (Sample shown at close of chapter.)

The information for each service—Sunday morning, Sunday evening, and Wednesday evening—should be written on the work sheets, using a different sheet for each service. When the work sheet is folded once lengthwise, it is the exact size of a standard sheet of typewriter paper (8½ by 11). The work sheets, with transferred information, should be placed in manila folders, a different folder used for each service. The manila folders should be marked "January, 1st Sun. A.M."; "January, 1st Sun. P.M."; "January, 1st Wed."; and so on.

There should be twelve to fifteen folders for each month, depending on the number of Sundays in the month. These twelve or fifteen folders should be placed in a larger folder, adequate in size to care for the resulting bulkiness. This plan gives a large, inclusive folder for each month in the year, January through December. Each of the twelve folders will have twelve to fifteen inside folders, with a work sheet for each individual folder.

The weekly folders and the weekly work sheets will now become the repository for ideas, clippings, references, illustrations, and incidents. Clippings can be dropped into the appropriate folder; references to books, magazines, and periodicals can be noted on the work sheet along with sprouting ideas and budding outlines. By keeping the preaching chart always before him at his desk, and by spending an hour each week in looking over the file, a minister will find that much of what he reads, sees, hears, or experiences in any way will begin to relate itself to some part of his preaching and teaching program.

He will not be like Old Mother Hubbard with a bare cupboard. Instead, when he comes to preach on any given Sunday, he may well be embarrassed by the generous flow of ideas and the accumulation of materials that beg for expression. The leftover material from the work sheets and files becomes a rich source of help for future sermons. The longer a minister uses such a plan, the greater its cumulative value.

MONTH, YEAR

	Event	A.M.	P.M.	Wed.
1st Week		————(Sun. date)	————(Sun. date)	————(Wed. date)
2nd Week		————	————	————
3rd Week		————	————	————
4th Week		————	————	————
5th Week		————	————	————

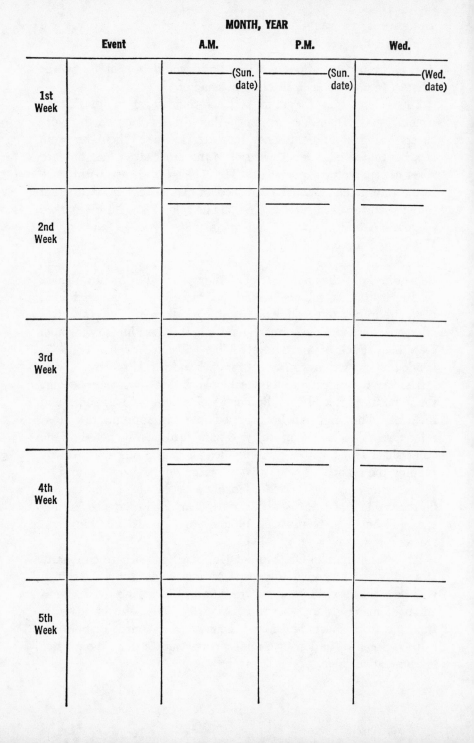

WORK SHEET

Suggested Subjects, Themes	Bible Text and References	
Word Study	Introduction	Outline
		BODY
Illustrations, Quotations, Clippings, References	I	
	II	
	III	
	IV	
	Conc.	

2
Reasons for the Plan

A broadcaster on a New England radio used to end his program with the words, "This is your friend and mine," and give his own name. A man should be a friend to himself as well as to other people. Jesus said that the second commandment was to love others as you love yourself. Then, intelligent Christian self-love would be the measure of love for others. A preaching program should be a "friend" to the congregation and to the preacher who uses it. Unless the plan is a friend to both, it will benefit neither in the long run.

Values in Planning

To begin, let it be stated that a planned preaching program *gives the Holy Spirit a better chance to do his work with and in the preacher*—the work of revealing the will and purpose of God as they relate to the sermon. Time was when it was believed that the Holy Spirit did his best work "without benefit of clergy," that is, instantaneously, with no forethought. No. The Holy Spirit prefers working with the preacher in the pulpit who has first given the Holy Spirit the opportunity to work in the preacher's study. The more diligent and devoted the preacher has been in his study, the more freedom the Holy Spirit has with the preacher in the pulpit.

Hans Klaus, one of the leaders in the revival movement in Germany, once gave a sharp answer to a young preacher who boasted that he never made preparation for preaching since he was confident of the Holy Spirit and knew that the Holy Spirit would give him, on the spot, what should be said. The old minister shook his head and said: "For fifty years I have been preaching the gospel, and only once has the Holy Spirit spoken to me while I was preaching. The Holy Spirit has often spoken to me as I was leaving the pulpit, and what he said was: 'Hans, you are lazy!' "

A second value in a planned preaching program is based on the need of a minister *to preach in the direction of the full gospel.* The word "direction" is used deliberately. No man can preach the "full" gospel. It is too great for our little minds to comprehend, to say nothing of preaching it. But, we must try; many do not.

Some years ago a friend left the pastorate of a large and useful church where he had been for ten years. His friends wondered why he left. His explanation was that each minister had one major emphasis to make. This emphasis, he contended, could be given and developed in a ten-year period. It was, then, to the welfare of the congregation that the minister move on and let another man come with a different emphasis, another emphasis that the people needed, and that the people would be poorer for not receiving.

It is not necessary that you agree entirely with that position in order to appreciate it. Different men do have different emphases. One minister with a distinguished career and a national reputation said that as he looked back over his ministry of forty years, he realized that he had only about eight sermons. There had been great variety in his approach and application, but actually his entire body of sermons could be grouped into about eight categories.

One thing is sure, most men repeat a great deal in their preaching. They preach, for the most part, from a few selected books of the Bible, and only from selected portions of those. The sermons by whatever title come out with about the same emphasis. In his fine little book, *The Making of the Sermon,* Robert J. McCracken tells about the deacon in a Scottish church who, week after week, had the same refrain in his prayers. He would pray, "O for the wings of a dove that I might fly away and be at rest." Week after tiring week the old man raised the same petition. Unable to stand the boring repetition any longer, a fellow worshiper was heard to groan, "Stick another feather in him, Lord, and let him go!" It might be well for a minister to remember that his people are not as patient as the Lord; they just might let him go, feather or no feather!

Again, the minister needs to plan his preaching because *it tends to inspire a teaching ministry*. It has been said that every sermon should have at least one idea! Members of the congregation would agree. All good preaching has a strong didactic element. No minister fulfils his office as preacher unless he has good solid teaching material in his sermons.

A minister who is recognized throughout his denomination as one of its most effective men, a man who has spent his entire professional ministry in one church, has contended that a minister can have the kind of church he wants after fifteen years with that church. If it is not as he wants it at first, he can grow it as he desires it. His brethren have differed with him on that. All the same, the statement does point up the need for and effectiveness of the preacher as teacher. It is certain that if the preacher is going to build, grow, mold, or create a different church from the one he finds when he is first made its pastor, he will have to do a great deal of teaching.

It is said repeatedly that congregations are uninformed; it is true. Not long ago a national magazine reported on a survey taken in "quite a proper congregation in a boulevard church located in a college section of a rather large city." What did the questionnaire reveal? Over a third of the people did not know that Nazareth was the town where Jesus was brought up. Nearly a fourth could not identify Calvary as the place of the death of Jesus. (These were all adult members!) Gethsemane "rang no bell" for 43 percent; 75 percent said they could attach no significance to the word "Pentecost"; one or more thought Amos was "the husband of Mary whom he brought back to life"; the Gospels were "meeting places for the apostles"; "Samaritans were angels"; "Zacchaeus was one of the minor prophets"; and "Elijah was a king or a disciple."

If that state of affairs exists in relation to simple scriptural information, what do you think would be the result of a test on the basic matters of doctrine and theology, or the implications of the gospel or present-day living in areas such as social, economic, and political?

In most churches there is a rather solid core in the congregation that returns Sunday after Sunday to the hour of worship. There should be a cumulative educational value to the services. Recently a man asked a question of a person in public life; there was silence. After a little while, the person who had asked the question said: "I could take your silence to any lawyer in this city and sue for slander!" There has been too much guilty silence on the part of preachers who ought to be teaching in and through their sermons.

Worthwhile Worship

Look further: a planned preaching program *aids in the building of a worthy service of worship*. This is important. The true worship of God is man's highest function and his greatest need. Ideally, people do not attend church to hear a sermon; they come to worship God. A worthy sermon will have a vital place in that experience.

The different parts of the service can be carefully chosen and wisely planned in relationship to each other. Calls to worship, responses, prayers, hymns, Scripture reading, anthems, sermons, preludes, postludes, interludes, silence, and meditation can be vital parts of a whole, "in [which] all the building fitly framed together groweth unto an holy temple in the Lord."

The needs of the people are too great for the sermon to assume full responsibility. There are few discoveries that will bring more comfort to the preacher than the knowledge that the various parts of the service, if carefully planned, earnestly prayed over, and effectively administered, will of themselves minister to the needs of the people. To know that God can, has, and will come to his people through these channels is knowledge that is "more precious than gold, yea than much fine gold."

Every person who has administered hours of worship knows that such a service, such an experience of worship, does not "just happen." It cannot be extemporized on the spot in a quickly thrown together "order of service." This kind cometh forth only through much prayer, effort, and planning.

A carefully planned program of preaching also *offers one of the best possibilities for growth and refreshment on the part of the minister himself*. No self-respecting preacher can be content when "the hungry sheep look up and are not fed." But, if the preacher is to feed the sheep entrusted to his care, he must be "like unto a man that is an householder, which bringeth forth out of his treasure things new and old." The preacher must look to his own storehouse, his own "treasure." How tragic, indeed, for a preacher to have to admit: "They made me keeper of the vineyards; but mine own vineyard have I not kept."

A man's intellectual life is always reflected in his preaching. These two are never kept in completely different compartments. If his preaching is a "hand to mouth" matter, or present-book-to-next-Sunday's-sermon, then nothing short of a startling miracle can produce an ordered, developed, and mature mind. However, if he has planned his preaching a year in advance, next Sunday's sermon need no longer place him under the undue tension expressed in the old children's game that has as its refrain: "coming, whether you're ready or not."

In his report for 1869–70, President Charles W. Eliot of Harvard referred to plans for the Harvard Divinity School. He said that the pulpits of this country would not be filled by geniuses; that if they were so filled there would be small use for theological schools. It was his conviction, he reported, that the pulpits would be filled by ordinary men of good and natural parts, but men who had been carefully trained for their special work. These men would need to be scholars by temperament, education, and by inveterate habit, "else their congregations will drain them dry in a year or two."

"Scholars by temperament," good; "scholars by education," excellent; "scholars by inveterate habit," imperative! That is, the pulpits need to be filled by men with such ingrained, fixed, channels of habit and study that they will be lifelong students.

Planned preaching *makes for timeliness in preaching*. This, of course, is just the opposite of what is often charged against planned preaching. It is frequently claimed that if you plan your preaching program a year in advance, you cannot take advantage of the needs of your people arising out of the circumstances they meet from day to day, the swiftly changing civic, social, economic, and political situations that appear upon the human horizon.

There are several answers to such a charge. One might say that it is not the business of the pulpit to be so much concerned with the rapidly changing scenes upon the human horizon as with the eternal and abiding scenes upon the divine horizon. But, the truth of the matter is that two seemingly contradictory points of view need not be contradictory at all. For, if one deals with the eternal and abiding scenes in any relevant way, he will have to do so in the context of the present human scene. "David served his own generation by the will of God." Of course, that was the one generation he could serve; if he served it well he might thereby serve other generations, also, but he had to serve his own or he would serve none. Certainly, it is through serving his own generation that he will be fulfilling the will of God for his life. It is just as sure that if the minister deals effectively with the issues on the human horizon, he will have to do so through the light and help that he gets from the divine horizon.

There is another point that needs to be made. One who conscientiously seeks to bring to his people the full gospel in his preaching program will be surprised to find how often that "full" gospel speaks directly to their immediate needs. It is also true that to be forewarned is to be forearmed. One reason we do not deal effectively with issues that arise suddenly is that we give no thought to the possibility that such issues may arise. When a man preaches from week to week, he never deals effectively with issues that arise from week to week. He does not do so because he is unprepared to do so, and it is too late for him to "load his gun and fire" on the spot. Instead, what he does is to deal with some subject that he can "lay violent hands upon," something that he has a little material on, a few illustrations to back up.

In contrast, the man who has his preaching program carefully planned, who has been doing careful study, preparing the soil, sowing, planting, transplanting, tending, fertilizing, cultivating, pruning, grafting, and selecting, is ready when the market calls. Such a man is able to harvest quickly that which is a credit to his labors and an honor to his God. He neither has to pass up the need because he cannot meet it, nor try to force-feed something to get it ready for next Sunday's market.

Saving Time

There is this, too, that can be said about planning your preaching program: *it saves time.* From the standpoint of conscious need on the part of most ministers, this should have been placed at the head of the list of values!

Surveys are constantly being made among ministers. From survey to survey the gripes and complaints vary, but there is one that reappears with every poll. It is that ministers are overworked; they do not have time to do their real work; their time is taken up with trivia; they cannot find time to study and prepare their sermons.

The preacher may find difficulty in convincing an efficiency expert that such is the case. It would be impossible for the minister to write out a job analysis or list a schedule of activities that would carry weight with anyone who has not been in the ministry; one who has requires no proof! To an outsider, the modern minister's complaint may be reminiscent of the old farmer who was sitting on his porch with this shoes off, his feet resting comfortably on the porch rail. A neighbor rushed over and shouted to the old man that his cow had gotten out and was eating up the garden corn, to which the old farmer replied: "I know it; I know it; but I can't do everything!"

But of the lack of time, the problem is still there and every preacher knows it.

It would be agreed that much time is wasted by the average minister. One way he wastes it is in deciding what he is going to preach on next Sunday. He chews his pencil and stares at his illiterate typewriter. He turns the leaves of his reluctant Bible; he flips the cards or pages containing dry "Ideas for Sermons"; he thumbs through his "Best Sermons" and wonders how they could be so designated. He begins to write; he wads the paper and tosses it in the wastebasket. He reads a chapter in the latest book club selection; he reaches for the *Reader's Digest;* he scans *The Christian Century* and *Christianity Today*. He gets an idea, works over it for a day and a half and finds that it "will not fly without flopping" and has to throw it away. Before he knows what has become of the time, it is Thursday morning and he seems no further along with next Sunday's sermon than he was on Monday morning. Painful? Yes. But true! And rare is the preacher who does not know it is true. The time we waste in deciding what we are going to preach, if properly utilized, would create masterpieces!

> Biting my truant pen,
>   Beating myself for spite,
> Fool, said my muse to me,
>   Look in thy heart, and write.[1]

Good advice. But it takes more than looking into the heart and mind to produce a worthwhile sermon; the heart and mind have to be fed. It is the preacher who has a well structured, long-range preaching plan, who has lived with the plan, has stoked his fires by constant and careful reading and diligent study, who finds, "My mind to me a kingdom is." To him each sermon in the future is like a choice watermelon that a farmer has marked in his field. He keeps his eye on it; week by week the melon grows and ripens on the vine. The farmer eagerly looks forward to a certain day, event, celebration, knowing that the watermelon will be ripe and ready to gladden the eye and delight the tastes of friends and loved ones.

Another value of a planned program of preaching that is similar to the one just discussed is this: *it compensates for interruptions.* A preacher wastes a lot of time deciding what he is going to preach about; he wastes time in other ways, too. But when allowance has been made for the wasted time, the fact still remains that a minister runs short of needed time. One of the reasons for this is the matter of interruptions.

A preacher cannot schedule his time to rule out all interruptions. He should not if he could; he could not if he would. In a very real sense, the more successful and efficient a minister is, the more interruptions he will have. It is possible for a minister to have too few interruptions. All he has to do is fail his people in their hour of need, to "strike out" whenever his city and community call upon him to perform a service, to ignore or be indifferent to every call of his denomination and fellow Christians, and very soon he will find that he is not being interrupted. In fact, he may well find that even his church hesitates to interrupt him for the regularly scheduled services, or even to ask that he cash his monthly salary check. His people will be so concerned that he not be disturbed that he will find himself without a church to disturb him!

So, one mark of a functioning minister is the number and type of interruptions he experiences.

What is an interruption and what is an opportunity for service? The answer depends more upon the minister than it does on the call or need. Now, surely, no good minister believes that his only task is to stay in his study until he goes to his pulpit and to come directly from his pulpit back to his study for an uninterrupted stay until he goes to his pulpit again. Neither does he expect that people will schedule their sorrows and other problems to always coincide with the days and hours that the preacher sets aside for counseling and visiting. Opportunities for service in his denomination and community will not always clear with his schedule before they knock on his door. No, let the preacher so plan his work and so respect that plan that these possible interruptions will, in reality, be considered privileges and opportunities.

Building a Library

Take another look: a planned preaching program will *assist a minister in building a worthy library*. Books are expensive; the minister's salary is relatively small. According to a recent survey, it is about at the bottom for all professions. A wise observation might be that the only thing more expensive for the minister than books is the absence of books.

What is his standard in buying books? How are the books selected? Men buy books according to authors, according to subject and title, on the basis of book reviews and advertisements, on the recommendation of friends, by the choice of book clubs, and by what seems to be popular consumption at the moment. If a book is at the top of the best-seller list, we are prone to feel that it has to be good, so we want to read it.

Any one of these methods of selection, certainly a combination of the methods, will put some good books in his library. However, the library may resemble what the man said about the Manhattan telephone directory: "There's quite a cast here, but no plot!"

One of the better ways to select and build a working library is in response to a well-planned, long-range preaching program. When a man is preaching from week to week, he cannot purchase books to assist him with his preaching. When he uses a long-range plan, he can. If he knows that he is going to preach a series of sermons on the prophets, the Ten Commandments, the apostles, the parables, the miracles, the Sermon on the Mount, the questions Jesus asked, or contrasts between the old and new morality, and if the series is planned for nine months ahead, he can buy two, a half-dozen, a dozen or more good books in that particular field. If the preacher adds to this list any good book, new or old, that he comes across, within a few years his library will be substantial on this subject.

Again, if a man plans his preaching according to the Christian Year, books can be purchased by seasons, festivals, days, and emphases. Or, if the plan follows the line of Christian doctrine, books can be bought that deal with great theological truths. In this and similar ways, a minister will build a library that is not only practical, but, at the same time, filled with books that are frigates to bear his mind and spirit to lands of gold.

Similar to the minister's need to build a worthy library is the need for him to find *sufficient incentive and encouragement to spend time in that library, once it is built*. A planned preaching program does this. This brings us back to the matter of the minister's being too busy to study. Books that remain on shelves do the minister little good. Books must be opened; they must be read and pondered and digested.

Absenteeism is taking a frightening toll on the nation's economy. On every working day an estimated 3,500,000 employees fail to show up for work. At the last count, absenteeism was costing

United States industry the staggering sum of $13,600,000,000 each year! [2]

What about absenteeism on the part of the preacher from his study? No reliable poll has been taken; no accurate estimate has been made. It is safe to say that the number of hours lost and the resulting paucity in sermon content and passion would be staggering, could it be shown in a Gallup Poll!

Why are preachers absent from their studies? That is simple— they are busy with other things. Calls upon their time and talents are numerous. The role of the present-day minister has changed. The modern minister is expected to do a score of things that his predecessor did not know existed. This is not the whole story, however.

The minister evaluates his work; he must do this. He has priorities. He does what he feels is most important or pressing first, and other things take their turns.

If the modern minister is guilty, let him face up to the truth that one reason he does not stay in his study and do mental work is that he would rather stay out of his study and do other kinds of work. He finds that easier! He finds it more satisfying; he feels that it is more rewarding. Why does he not find satisfaction and fulfilment through intellectual work in his study? He sees little result from his labors. He is unable to produce, to create. If he calls upon six individuals in an afternoon, he may see two of those individuals in church on the following Sunday. It is not so easy for him to see the results of his mental activity!

Preachers will not stay in their studies and work from a sheer sense of duty; they must find enjoyment in their work. There must be a feeling of fulfilment, of accomplishment, of satisfaction. This will come through ordered work, planned study, accumulated skills and ability, and growth in knowledge and understanding.

Developing Thought

Another result of the planned preaching program is the *aid that it gives to the unconscious.* By this is meant all that which goes on in the mind below the floor of conscious attention. In discussing the "unconscious mind" as the preacher's ally, Halford E. Luccock once said, "Without it, the audacious enterprise of preaching week after week, year after year, in the same place, would be so formidable as to be terrifying." [3]

There are certain organs of the body that work on twenty-four hour shifts. Whether you are awake or sleeping, they continue to perform their functions. The heart, the lungs, and the brain are in this group. They are never inactive.

The unconscious mind, for example, never sleeps. It is a willing worker, but it insists on working according to rules. Give it a proper assignment, the necessary raw products and questions to feed upon, and plenty of time, and it will bring you strange and wonderful things from the past. It can select, combine, deduct, foresee, analyze, but it must be given time. It despises deadlines and instant results. This is why long-range planning is absolutely essential if the preacher would make full use of this resource. The man who works from week to week, who only decides this Thursday what he is going to preach next Sunday morning, is making practically no use whatever of this willing servant.

Look at a final value of the planned preaching program: it *helps the preacher to develop a writing ministry.* Two generalizations can be made with a fair degree of assurance. First, whatever the pastor publishes, he first will have preached to his people. It may not, probably will not, be published in just the form that he preached it, but the wise can recognize the similarity! Second, with proper planning and discipline, most ministers can see their efforts in print. It is a worthy ambition for a minister to have. Why should he not want to extend his ministry? If he does not so desire, what is wrong with his desiring apparatus? If what he has said to his own people has been helpful to them, the chances are that it would be helpful to other people.

His first efforts, possibly his last efforts, will be modest. This should not deter him. A thing that is worth doing is worth doing even poorly! If it is worth doing, it ought to be done. If a person waits until he can do excellently the thing that needs to be done, he will never be found among the ranks of those who do what ought to be done. Let the preacher write!

But, if the busy pastor is to write, he has to engage in long-range planning. If he does this, practically everything that has been written in this chapter will assist him. He will have the necessary intellectual qualifications; he can develop the necessary writing skills; there will be time. Peter Grothe once said of Sargent Shriver, "Still in his forties, Sargent Shriver had led the kind of life that undoubtedly has induced the recording angels to learn short-hand." [4] No one has heard the recording angels complain. Let the preacher crowd his schedule.

Let him plan his preaching program at least a year in advance. Let him include in that program, well along in the year, a series of ten or twelve sermons of vital interest and helpful concern. Let him take half of the number for one year and half for the second year. Let him give to that series the kind of hard work, wide reading and research, earnest prayer, and careful skill that each of his sermons should receive, and see what happens. In all probability, he will be able to find a publisher; but if he does not, his people who hear the sermons will be so grateful that the preacher will not greatly care whether the sermons are published or not! This will show the rewarding result of a planned preaching program.

3
A Garment of Celebration

A comprehensive and adequate preaching plan needs to give careful attention to the traditional Christian Year. Also called "The Church Year," "The Christian Calendar," "The Church Calendar," and "The Liturgical Calendar," it is a term whose full intent and purpose is difficult to define. It is easier to describe its function.

The term is used to designate the effort to Christianize certain seasons and days of the year for the purpose of worship. The breakdown of the year in this way dramatizes and celebrates the chief events in the life of Christ and in his gospel regularly so that these events will contribute to the life of the body of Christ and its members. It has been called "a compass whose needle always points to Christ," or "the garment of celebration worn by the churches through the centuries."

The roots of the Christian year date farther back than the Christian movement itself. It was developed unconsciously by the apostles and their immediate successors, and its basic structure was formed by the established church in the early centuries. Since the Reformation there have been changes in the branches of the original structure, and new branches have been added; changes are still taking place. But the basic form of the Christian Year is much as it was centuries ago.

Such a plan has several advantages. It is ancient. It has stood the test of use. More Christian denominations and churches follow the plan of the Christian Year in their worship than any other pattern. Furthermore, the Christian Year provides the churches and individual Christians with a planned, purposeful system of lessons that draw upon and seek to familiarize the worshiper with the whole Word of God. It aims at the teaching and the preaching of the whole gospel. It calls attention to the lives and contributions of New Testament Christians and to individual Christian saints and martyrs who have lived since New Testament times, and it encourages present-day Christians to emulate these.

Utilization

All denominations make some use of the Christian Year; some make more use of it than others. Some who do use it are unaware that they do so—somewhat like the girl who was surprised to learn that she had been speaking prose all her life!

All Christian groups, with very few exceptions, observe Sunday, the Lord's Day. Sunday is the foundation stone of the Christian year. Again, nearly all groups observe Christmas and Easter. These two Christian festivals are basic to the Christian Year. There is agreement on and mutual participation in the three Christian festivals that are fundamentally important to the Christian Year.

There is another sense in which Christians are united in a mutual observance of the year. The great events in the life of Christ and in his gospel are taught and proclaimed. These events may not be observed according to a schedule as Christmas, Easter, and Sunday are, but they are a part of the truth taught and proclaimed by the "freest" of the "free" churches.

All Christian groups believe in and proclaim the great doctrine of the Holy Spirit. The proclamation and emphasis may not take place on the day designated "Pentecost Sunday," but it is done. And, the strictest liturgical churches do not limit their observance and proclamation to "Pentecost Sunday." The truths of the Advent season are proclaimed—Christ's coming in Bethlehem, his final coming as judge, his present comings to his people in their need.

Also, the showing forth of God's grace through the revelation of his Son's humanity and the implications of this for man's redemption are proclaimed in our churches, even though we may not know the meaning of the word "Epiphany." The same may be said for other seasons and emphases of the Christian Year. Since these authentic and greatly cherished events in the life of our Lord are taught and proclaimed by all of his followers, might there not be advantages in doing them in unison at stated and definite times—that is, by observing the Christian Year?

Explanation

Where the Christian Year is not more fully used, could it be because many ministers do not know about it? How can we cooperatively use a calendar that we do not know about? Millions have grown up in a tradition that did not use the Christian Year, that made no provision for teaching about it or practicing it in the fellowship of the church. Remember when Paul asked the Ephesians: "Did you receive the Holy Spirit when you believed?" Back came the answer: "No, we have never even heard that there is a Holy Spirit." Paraphrase that and see how it looks: "Do you use the Christian Year in your preaching program?" Many preachers might truthfully answer: "No, I have never even heard that there was a Christian Year."

Another reason the Christian Year is not more widely used is this: it is condemned on the basis of "guilt by association." It is easy to react against a form because it is used by a particular group or denomination, especially if it is misused. When the father demanded to know why the boys were scuffling on the floor, the older boy said: "Well, Dad, so far as I can tell, it all started when Bill fought back." The position we take on the Christian Year may be one of "fighting back"—"*re*acting" rather than acting.

Think, for example, of symbols used in worship. Some groups in certain areas have taken a strong position against the use of the cross. Is this due to a solid doctrinal conviction or is it due, at least in part, to a reaction against what we feel to be a misuse of the symbol by others? Or, if we are opposed to planned Scripture lessons, is it due to the fact that we have a different plan that is superior, or is our opposition due to a reaction against anything that suggests "liturgy" or "formalism" as practiced by others?

Again, give thought to anniversaries. There may be outright

antagonism against honoring anniversaries of apostles or other saints. "Saint's days? Indeed! Sheer popery!" Yet, the antagonism could scarcely be due to opposition against anniversaries as such. There is no opposition to observing the anniversaries of Washington, Lincoln, or St. Valentine. A person can be patriotic without giving any attention to the anniversaries of Washington and Lincoln, romantic without celebrating St. Valentine's Day, and religious without giving attention to St. Paul's Day. Still, is it not possible that there might be more spiritual help in the proper observance of St. John's Day than in an equally fitting observance of Lincoln's Day?

Occasions and symbols have been corrupted. The strongest exponent of tradition and liturgy would admit it. The same may be said for Christmas and Easter; it is one of our constant complaints. Still, we continue to observe the birth and resurrection of Christ on these days. These two came into the Christian Year partly to offset other corrupt practices that were being observed at these times. We are probably right in feeling that corruption is no reason for giving up a proper observance of these days—rather, an added incentive for continuing.

This is not to say that our churches should make a complete about-face and begin observing, in wholesale fashion, every day in the year for some saint—"saints preserve us!" Nor is the point being made that we should go overboard for signs and symbols, no more than we should take the steeples from the top of our churches and the "Do This in Remembrance of Me" from our communion tables. The emphasis is only that we ought to take advantage of the blessing a proper use of the Christian Year can bring to a preaching program.

Content

The Christian Year is divided into two main sections of approximately equal length. The first section is spoken of as the *Lord's half year,* or the section in which God takes the initiative. It includes Advent, Christmas, Epiphany, Lent, Easter, Ascension, and Pentecost. (Sometimes Pentecost is listed with the second half of the year.) The second section of the Christian Year is known as the *church's half year*, the human answer to the divine initiative, or man's response to God's action. The season begins with the festival of the Trinity (unless Pentecost is included and stands at the beginning) and runs to the beginning of Advent. The season is devoted to Christian instruction, growth, and initiative. It embraces none of the great religious festivals.

Advent

The Christian Year opens with the Advent season. Advent means "coming" or "arrival." The season emphasizes expectancy and preparation—expectancy of the coming of Christ and preparation for his coming. Advent begins on the Sunday closest to November 30, St. Andrew's Day, and continues for a total of four Sundays. The four Sundays emphasize in order his coming through accents upon creation, the Bible, the prophets, and the Forerunner, John the Baptist. His first coming as a baby in Bethlehem, his final coming as judge of the quick and the dead, and his repeated comings to his people in their experiences of need, are all part of the proclamation of Advent. The color for Advent is purple; it speaks of penitence and is associated with Christ as King, purple being a royal color.

Advent is one of the chief festivals today. It has not always been so. More emphasis was placed upon the ministry, death, and resurrection of Christ in the early stages of church history. It was considered pagan to observe birthdays. Martyrdom caused the church to celebrate the date of death rather than the date of birth of the saints. The origin of Advent was probably in Gaul, possibly Spain or Italy. It was being celebrated in these places by the fifth century, and in the sixth century was given a permanent place in the church calendar by Gregory the Great. It was in the ninth century that it took its present form and place.

Christmastide

Christmastide is the next celebration in the Christian Year and includes from one to two Sundays, depending on the day of the week that Christmas Day falls upon. Christmastide is a twelve-day festival, beginning on Christmas Eve. The emphasis is the incarnation and its relation to the Christian hope. The color used is white, suggesting godhead, purity, joy, and victory.

A separate celebration for the birth of Christ did not appear before the fourth century; until this time it was combined with the celebration of Epiphany, traditionally the time of the baptism of Jesus. The name "Christmas" came into use in the twelfth century; it was a contraction of "Christ's mass." There was serious doubt as to the exact date of the birth of Christ. December 25 does not appear in records as the birth date before the middle of the third century. It seems that, either consciously or unconsciously, this particular date was chosen to help offset pagan festivals and practice.

Epiphany

Epiphany means "manifestation" or "appearance." Attention in the celebration is given to the coming of the Wise Men, the baptism of Jesus, and the first miracle—the turning of the water into wine at the wedding feast in Cana. The season begins on January 6, the traditional date of the baptism of Jesus, and continues for a period of from four to nine weeks, depending on the date of Easter. The accent in the season is on Jesus Christ as the revealer of God to men. The missionary and evangelistic notes are appropriate. The color is green and stands for life and growth.

As stated above, Christmas and Epiphany were for a time combined. When the seasons were separated, Christmas was moved to December 25, and Epiphany remained at January 6. The latter probably arose in the Eastern Church first with the sole emphasis upon the baptism of Jesus. Later it took on the note of the nativity through its association with the coming of the Wise Men. In many sections, even in America, Epiphany is still called "Old Christmas."

Lent

The beginning of Lent is Ash Wednesday (in memory of the Old Testament phrase, "sackcloth and ashes," suggesting deep sorrow and penitence), and continues for forty days excluding Sundays prior to Easter. The word "Lent" probably comes from the Anglo-Saxon word "lencten," meaning spring. The season calls attention to Christ's temptation in the wilderness and its notes are those of self-examination, penitence, devotion, and renewal.

Two weeks in Lent are given special significance. The first is Passion Week. It runs from Passion Sunday, two Sundays before Easter, through Palm Sunday Eve. The second special week in Lent is Holy Week and is from Palm Sunday, one Sunday before Easter, through Easter Eve. There are special days in Holy Week: Palm Sunday, Maundy Thursday (*Maundy* is derived from the Latin for "command," from Christ's command to his disciples in the Upper Room on Thursday evening before his crucifixion on Friday), and Good Friday, emphasizing the death of Christ. The color for Lent is purple, the same as for Advent. The one exception is Good Friday, whose color is black, signifying death.

A form of Lent, of preparation for Easter, was practiced as early as the second century. At first it was for a period of forty hours, equal to the time Christ spent in the tomb. Then the time was lengthened to six days, and finally to forty days, the forty days representing the forty years the children of Israel spent in the wilderness, the forty days Moses spent on the mount, the forty days Jesus was in the wilderness, and the forty hours he spent in the tomb. "Sundays *in* Lent" indicates that Sundays are not actually a part of Lent. Sunday is a feast day, a "Little Easter," always; therefore, only weekdays are counted in Lent.

Eastertide

This great season in the Christian Year begins with Easter Sunday and continues for fifty days until Pentecost. It was the earliest of the seasons in point of development. Its great event is the risen Christ. The risen Christ and the reigning Lord are the bugle notes that are sounded throughout the season. Easter is the most important of all the Christian celebrations. It was this that transformed the disciples from doubting, fearful men into a triumphant band; it transformed the Passover celebration into the resurrection celebration; it brought into being the church. The color is white, the same as for

Christmas, signifying godhead, joy, and victory. The season includes Ascension Day and Ascension Sunday. Ascension Day is forty days after the resurrection. The date of Easter was set by the Council of Nicaea in A.D. 325. It falls on the first Sunday after the first full moon that occurs on or after March 21. Easter, therefore, may be anywhere between March 22 and April 25.

Pentecost

Pentecost begins on the fiftieth day after Easter, the seventh Sunday. It lasts from twelve to seventeen Sundays. The season emphasizes the coming of the Holy Spirit to the followers of Jesus gathered in Jerusalem. It is usually called "The Birthday of the Church." It is one of the very important seasons of the church and was celebrated early in the life of the church. The emphasis throughout the church is one of missions and victory. The color is red, symbolizing the tongues as of fire that descended upon the disciples. This marks the close of the first half of the Christian Year. (The entire second half of the Christian Year is often lumped together in the one season of "Trinitytide.")

Kingdomtide

This is the newest of the seasons, dating no farther back than the late thirties; there are many Protestant groups that have not accepted it.

The arrangement suggested here eliminates the long and traditional Trinity season, a season that included from twenty-three to twenty-nine Sundays. While the newer plan breaks with tradition, there does seem to be wisdom in observing the two seasons, Pentecost and Kingdomtide. The longer and greater emphasis upon Pentecost gives opportunity to accent the place of the Holy Spirit and the church. The season of Kingdomtide gives place for due attention to the eternal presence of Christ and his kingship, with the parallel emphasis upon man's stewardship. Its color is green or white.

The season begins on the last Sunday in August and runs to Advent. Its emphasis is the kingship of Christ. The note is on his

kingdom as it challenges men in their daily lives and every area
of their existence.

And so the Christian Year comes to a close and begins again. It
can be said with Browning, "That after Last, return the First, though
a wide compass round be fetched." The season has been attractively
set forth in verse by Katherine Hankey:

> Advent tells us Christ is near;
> Christmas tells us Christ is here.
> In Epiphany we trace
> All the glory of his grace.
>
> Then three Sundays will prepare
> For the time of fast and prayer,
> That, with hearts made penitent
> We may keep a faithful Lent.
>
> Holy Week and Easter then
> Tell who died and rose again:
> O that happy Easter Day!
> "Christ is risen indeed," we say.
>
> Yes, and Christ ascended, too,
> To prepare a place for you;
> So we give him special praise
> After those great forty days.
>
> Then He sent the Holy Ghost
> On the day of Pentecost,
> With us ever to abide;
> Well may we keep Whitsuntide.
>
> Last of all, we humbly sing
> Glory to our God and King,
> Glory to the one in three,
> On the feast of Trinity.[1]

4

Formation of the Christian Year

Christianity did not grow up in a vacuum. It came into a culture that had well-formulated religious practices. The earliest followers of Jesus were Jews with a rich heritage. They were heirs of promise, the descendants of Abraham, Isaac, and Jacob.

Jesus went to the synagogue on the sabbath day. He made it clear that he came to fulfil the Hebrew law, not to destroy it. His disciples worshiped in the Temple, and Paul made use of the synagogues in his missionary efforts. This rich heritage and these well-formulated customs not only influenced the early followers of Jesus in their own religious habits and experiences but also influenced their teaching and leadership of the Gentiles who joined the Christian movement.

The Greco-Roman world of which the early Christians were citizens, as well as "strangers and sojourners," had its gods, shrines, and temples. It had its days, seasons, and festivals for religious observance. Paul said to the Athenians: "I see you are very religious." As the Gentiles began to come into the churches, a problem was created. The challenge was to change gods for all points future! But, pagan habits and customs were hard to leave behind. The Christians' command was not to conform but to be transformed. The work of the transformation and sublimation began. It went forward with astounding speed and thoroughness.

Transformation

Sunday is the first of all the great observances of the Christian

Year. The transformation of the Jewish sabbath into Sunday, the "Lord's Day," was no small accomplishment. It is difficult for a present-day Christian to understand how sacred the sabbath was to the Jew. He said that God made the day and hallowed it, that God himself rested upon the sabbath, and that he commanded that the day be kept. Yet, the Jewish sabbath was transformed into Sunday, the "Lord's Day."

How was it done? Christians said that Christ rose on the first day of the week, not the seventh. Christ appeared to his disciples on the first day. After a week, he reappeared to them on the first day. In Troas, Paul met with the brethren to break bread on this day; he instructed that on the first day they should "lay by them in store as God has prospered them." On the Isle of Patmos, John was "in the Spirit on the Lord's day." Sunday came to be known as a "Little Easter," for every Lord's Day was a celebration of the resurrection of Christ. It was as if Christ had said of this day, "Do this in remembrance of me." The day was transformed.

The *Passover* was a time of joyous celebration for the Jews. It kept ever before them the mighty acts of God in delivering them from Pharaoh, and marked the time when the angel of death passed over them and killed the Egyptians. But the Christian saw a greater act of God when he marked the doorpost of their sinful lives with the sacrificial love of Christ revealed at Calvary. The death of the Passover was transformed into the life of the resurrection. The Jewish Passover was transformed into the Christian Easter. The act of transformation is even clearer when it is realized that the word "Easter" is itself marked with sublimation and transformation, for it probably comes from the old Teutonic goddess Estre, goddess of spring and dawn.

Pentecost, the Feast of Weeks, came fifty days after the Passover. For the Jews, it was a time of thanksgiving; it marked the first of the harvest. It also marked the giving of the Ten Commandments and the Torah. No wonder it was a time of celebration for the Jews! But, it marked a time of celebration for the Christian, also. The Christian was grateful for the Law and the first fruits and the teachings, but he was even more grateful for the Holy Spirit of God who had come upon the little band of disciples in Jerusalem on the day of Pentecost. As a result three thousand were added to their number.

So, Pentecost was invested with new meaning. In some cases even the word was changed to "Whitsunday," or "White Sunday," from the white baptismal robes that the candidates wore. Voldi, a character in Lloyd Douglas' story *The Big Fisherman*, said that while he could not describe the voice of Jesus, it was a unifying voice. It had the power to convert a great crowd of distrustful strangers into a tight little group of blood brothers. That is what Pentecost meant to the early disciples.

Other dates and seasons felt the lifting and transforming power of the living God; more and more time yielded to the Lord of history. As time yielded, it found itself caught up into a great unifying purpose. The past and present and future were one fabric, for it was ruled by one who is the same yesterday, today, and forever. Time itself was being redeemed, and so, the second principle emerges.

Consecration

The second principle at work in the formation of the Christian Year was consecration. The word means "to make or declare sacred, by certain ceremonies or rites; to appropriate to sacred uses; to set apart; to devote to a high purpose; to dedicate." This process is evident throughout the development of the Christian Year.

The holy days and seasons had to be allied to and yet separate from other seasons and days. If the separation was too great, there would be no help. If the similarity between the "holy" and the "secular" was too great, there could be no redemption. The Christian Year had to be in the world; it could not be of the world. It had to stand above the secular or it could not give life; it had to stand close to the secular or it could not reach it. The Christian Year had to be different but not too different for nature's daily need.

This principle of consecration could be abused; it occasionally was. But corrupted practices do not necessarily condemn worthy principles. The fact that hermits have separated themselves from the call of needy humanity does not alter the fact that it is necessary to withdraw from men occasionally if you would help men repeatedly. Jesus believed in and practiced withdrawal.

Sunday is different from Monday; Christmas is different from the Fourth of July; the church is different from the football stadium; the Bible is not the same as *Lady Chatterley's Lover*; the cross is not the same as the hammer and sickle; the communion cup is different from the cocktail glass. The Christian Year undertakes to consecrate, to set apart days and seasons for sacred purposes—for the redemption of the secular days and seasons.

One great danger of present thinking can be diminished by proper use of the Christian Year. This is the belief that by destroying emphasis on particular days and seasons as being sacred, you thereby make all days and seasons sacred. It is a strange argument that says the way to consecrate the secular is to forsake a sense of the church as sacred. That is like saying the way to fight Indians on the frontier would have been to burn down the fort where the ammunition was stored and from which the men went forth to fight. No! That way madness lies. There must be a home base, a center of operations. If all days are to be sacred, some particular days must be sacred. The particular must be magnified before the general can be glorified. The Christian Year recognizes the validity of the principle of consecration.

Regularity

Similar to the reasons for the consecration of certain days and seasons is the reason for regularity in observing certain days and seasons. If you are to obey Paul's injunction to pray at all times without ceasing, you will have to pray at certain times with regularity. To forsake the regularity of prayer at certain times on the basis that it deemphasizes constancy in prayer at all times is to fly in the face of psychological laws as well as in the face of scriptural teachings.

Run that truth out in several directions. You celebrate your wedding anniversary once each year, not because it is the only day in the year when you are grateful for your companion, but because you are always grateful for her. This is the way to become more grateful every day in the year. An institution observes Founders' Day once each year because it is grateful for and influenced by the contributions and sacrifices of its founders every day.

In like manner, the Christian Year sets forth the principle of regularity. We celebrate Christmas once each year, but not in order that we may forget the incarnation for the rest of the year. We celebrate the resurrection each Easter, but not because it is the only time when we are grateful for the triumph of Christ. No, the celebration on certain days with regularity is indicative of our gratitude throughout the entire year, and because we know that special celebration on one day will magnify the importance of the doctrine for every day. The same is true for each great event in the life of Christ, each great doctrine affirmed by the gospel and emphasized by the Christian Year.

Completeness

Novelist Lloyd Douglas is reported to have said that he wrote his book *The Robe,* a story dealing with Christ and his early followers, because he had never been satisfied with the creed that puts only a comma between the birth and the passion of Christ: "Born of the Virgin Mary, suffered under Pontius Pilate."

The Christian Year seeks to emphasize the completeness, the wholeness of the gospel. That cannot be done perfectly; the gospel is too great for our little minds and our short days. But an earnest effort can be made, and the Christian Year helps with that effort.

Attention has been called to Christmas and Easter, to the birth and resurrection of Christ. These are the great axes upon which the life of Jesus and the "mighty works of God" revolve, and practically all Christian groups observe these dates. But that is not enough; God did not think so. If it had been enough, we would have only the record of his birth and resurrection. We have more, much more. The gospel includes also the revelation of Christ as God's Son and Saviour of men. It reveals his temptations and suffering, his ascension as reigning Lord over the universe, his eternal presence through the Holy Spirit, and his promise to come again as judge of the quick and the dead.

The Christian Year emphasizes these great doctrines by majoring on seven great seasons: Advent, Christmas, Epiphany, Lent, Easter, Pentecost, Trinity (and/or Kingdomtide). The Christian Year, then, gives a framework within which the full gospel may be approached. The framework offers wholeness and specifics, variety and balance. There is provision for giving due attention to God and man, to the here and now as well as to the hereafter. Within the Christian Year there is an offer of "God's plenty."

In addition to a framework for proclamation, the Christian Year suggests Scripture lessons for the public worship services for each Sunday in the year. This material is called a lectionary. The selections come from the Old and New Testaments. They are chosen with the particular seasons in mind, and are drawn from different books of the Bible so that the major parts of the whole Bible can be read with meaningful continuity. Appropriate music may be selected. Many churches use different colors in the services, colors that are associated with the great gospel themes being emphasized. In these ways the gospel is proclaimed and received not just through hearing but through sight as well. The emphasis throughout the year is upon completeness.

It would be difficult to overemphasize the importance of this. When heresy has reared its ugly head, it has usually been due to an incomplete presentation of the gospel. It is not so much that what was taught has been false, although there was some of this. Usually, it was due to an overemphasis upon one truth of the gospel at the expense of some other doctrine of the Bible. One of the great concerns of the Christian Year is to obey the words of Christ when he said: "Teach them all things whatsoever I have commanded you."

Celebration

In *The Celebration of the Gospel*, Quillian, Hardin, and White make the point that Christian worship is always celebration because victory is the one true basis of worship. God has won the victory

over death and for life in and through Jesus Christ. The telling of
this victory is called the gospel (good news). Christian worship,
then, however solemn or exuberant, however simple or elaborate,
has its meaning in the victorious love of God. Therefore, a Christian
funeral is as surely celebration as is the Christian marriage service,
and a quiet family prayer in the evening as surely as a great communion service on Easter Day. Whatever is done in Christian worship is done as participation in God's victory through Christ.

In the book referred to above, the authors imaginatively re-
construct a Fourth of July celebration. There were parades, memorial services, invocations, patriotic addresses, games, fireworks, and
picnic lunches. Various groups march in the parade; they lay a
wreath at the foot of the monument to the honored dead; the flag is
raised in the park while all stand at attention and the national
anthem is played. Some noted citizen brings a stirring address re-
minding the crowd of the brave deeds performed by the heroes.
Following these formal ceremonies, the crowd breaks up for informal but corporate festivities.

When the day's activities are viewed objectively and carefully
analyzed, three essential aspects of the celebration stand out. There
was *remembrance*. This remembrance dipped into the past and
reached forward to the future. Light received from both directions
focused its beams upon the present. There was *thanksgiving*, gratitude to God for his guiding care and to the fathers for their faithfulness to duty. And, finally, there was *rededication*. In the light of
their thankfulness to God and forefathers, they gave themselves
anew to those ideals and principles which had made the day and
events possible.

These are the elements of true worship: remembrance, thanksgiving, and rededication. In such an experience the worshiper does
not stand alone. Obviously, this kind of experience is impossible for
the individual in isolation. The full significance of worship has to
take place in the community, within the "body of Christ." The
Christian Year sets before the community of the faithful the events
in the life of Christ; it calls upon the faithful to remember these

events, to be thankful, and to dedicate themselves to the fulfilment of the meaning of these events.

Anticipation

A necessary principle in the formation of the Christian Year was anticipation. The year gives more time to Advent than it does to Christmas; Lent stretches over a longer period of time than does the resurrection. Why is this? Anticipation and preparation are required if the nativity and the resurrection are to be experienced. The Bible is very sure of this. Its notes are loud and clear, "Prepare ye the way of the Lord." The prayer of an anonymous worshiper voices it:

O God, who didst prepare of old the minds and hearts of men for the coming of thy Son, and whose spirit ever worketh to illumine our darkened lives with the light of thy gospel: prepare now our minds and hearts, we beseech thee, that Christ may dwell within us, and ever reign in our thoughts and affections as the king of love, and the very Prince of Peace, for his sake. Amen.

Psychologically, as well as scripturally and historically, anticipation is a good thing. Just as nature prepares the body of the mother for the great event of a child's conception and birth, so spiritual births and rebirths have to be anticipated.

After the resurrection Christ appeared to those who were ready to see him. Those who were prepared to see him saw him; others did not see him. He appeared to Mary but not to Salome; Peter saw him, but Herod did not. In this, as in other ways, he seems to be the same "yesterday, today, and forever." He is realized by those who have anticipated his coming. The Christian Year anticipates every celebrated major event in the life of Christ. It calls upon believers to prepare.

> Go, preach, the kingdom is at hand,
>   The King is at the gate,
> Go, sound the news in every land,
>   He comes for whom you wait.[1]

Identification

A final principle that operated in the formation of the Christian Year was identification.

Ours is a historical religion. The redeeming God came in the form of Jesus of Nazareth; he lived in time and in space. "The word became flesh and dwelt among us." He had a name and an address. He lived through the stages of infancy, childhood, youth, and maturity. He experienced human life as it was lived in Palestine in the first century. He knew peace and anguish, trouble and triumph; he had family and friends, enemies and neighbors. "He was tempted in all points as we are tempted." But, although his life was lived out in time, it had a significance that transcended time. Events that took place on the stage of human history witnessed spiritual realities that were above history.

The apostle Paul was very sure that when Christ was preached, the result was more than something said. A true sermon was a deed done. To preach the gospel was to get God into action on the stage of history.

Says Donald G. Miller:

To preach is to become part of a dynamic event wherein the living, redeeming God reproduces his act of redemption in a living encounter with men through the preacher. True preaching is an extension of the Incarnation into the contemporary moment, the transfiguring of the Cross and the Resurrection from ancient facts of remote past into living realities of the present. A sermon is an act wherein the crucified, risen Lord personally confronts men either to save or to judge them.[2]

Then, any plan or program of preaching that will help a minister reproduce this divine event is to be welcomed. The Christian Year will do this, for it helps the preacher more nearly proclaim the full, whole, complete gospel. There is more, however. The very celebration of these events in the life of Christ—events that are spotlighted, consecrated, and regularized in the Christian Year—if they are done in spirit and in truth, bring God redemptively into the worship experience.

As the human life of Jesus unfolds through the Christian Year, from Advent through Easter and Pentecost, our lives are caught up in the procession. We are impressed with the similarity between his life and ours, yet we are shocked at the contrast between the way he lived his life and the way we live ours. His life unfurls before us: helpless infancy, disciplined and obedient youth, work and growth, choice and temptation, vocation and ministry, Holy Week and resurrection. It is all there to see and, if we dare, experience! We begin to understand as season after season, year after year, we see Christ tempted, betrayed, crucified, buried, raised, and glorified before our very eyes, as Paul would put it! We vicariously identify with him.[3]

Walter Marshall Horton wrote of a man who had been a delegate to the International Missionary Council at Madras in 1938 that the meeting made a deep impression on the delegate. When he returned home, he tried to persuade his friends to buy small globes. He wanted his friends to hold these globes in their hands once each day, as they slowly and reverently repeated the Lord's prayer, "Thy will be done on earth."

This incident is akin to the principles involved in the formation of the Christian Year. The world is held so that the rays from the life of Christ and his gospel may fall full upon it, and the worshiper says: "Thy will be done . . . Thy kingdom come."

5

Preaching by
the Christian Year

(PLAN I)

Much of what passes for preaching today would not be recognized as such if compared to primitive preaching. To attempt to duplicate the forms and language used by Peter and Paul would, admittedly, be a denial of the very spirit of the gospel. However, it is doubtful whether anything can rightly be called Christian preaching which does not concern itself with certain basic truths.

C. H. Dodd has outlined the apostles' messages in his widely used book, *The Apostolic Preaching.*[1] Here, in even briefer outline form, is the substance of early preaching.

First, a new age had now dawned. This day had been prophesied by the prophets; all the prophets from Samuel on foresaw the present events. They saw that after long centuries of waiting, God would visit his people. The preachers declared that that messianic age had now arrived. (Acts 2:16; 3:18, 24).

Second, this event had come about through the life and death and resurrection of Jesus. The apostles repeatedly affirmed that all this was by "the determinate counsel and foreknowledge of God." Christ descended from David; he was accredited by the people with being able to perform works of power and, therefore, signs of God. His death was in keeping with the plan and foreknowledge of God, but he was killed by men who disagreed with the Law. God raised him up, and the apostles were witnesses of it. (Acts 2:30-31; 3:22-23; 3:13-14; 4:10).

Third, by the power of the resurrection, Jesus had been exalted to the right hand of the throne of God; he was now the Messiah of

44

the new Jerusalem. "God has made him Lord and Christ." He was
rejected by the builders, but God had now made him the head of
the corner. (Acts 2:33–36; 3:13; 4:2; 5:13).

Fourth, the present power of the Holy Spirit within the church
was the sign of Christ's presence and power. God promised this
through his servant Joel. The apostles declared that they were witnesses of these things. So was the Holy Spirit, which God had given
to all who obeyed him. (Acts 2:17–21, 33; 5:32).

Fifth, this new messianic age would soon reach its fulfilment in
the return of Christ. For Christ had been appointed by God as judge
of the quick and dead. (Acts 3:21; 10:42).

Sixth, and finally, this preaching closed with an appeal to
repentance, the offer of forgiveness, and the promise of Holy Spirit
and life in the age to come. The promise was not only to those
present but to their children and to all who were afar off, even to
all those whom the Lord God would call. There was no other name
under heaven given to men whereby they might be saved. (Acts 2:
38–39; 3:19,25–26; 4:12; 5:31; 10:43).

This is the "kerygma," the "preaching" of the apostles—not the act
of preaching, but the message preached, or *what* the apostles
preached. It is impossible and unnecessary here to enter into a discussion of where the line can be drawn between the "preaching"
and the "teaching," (kerygma and didaché). Whether the first was
always and only to the unconverted and the second only and always
to the church, it is difficult to say. We do not know where one began
to be minimized and the other magnified. But when the line between the two has been drawn, it has been drawn too tightly.

The purpose here is to show how by following carefully the
Christian Year a minister will proclaim faithfully the great truths
preached by the apostles. Indeed, as the seven great seasons of the
Christian Year are studied, it is difficult to avoid the conclusion that
the formation of the calendar was mainly for the purpose of
guaranteeing the continuance of the kerygma.

It is an exhilarating experience to come upon a man in the mid-
twentieth century who boldly, unapologetically, and with great
effectiveness champions this position. Such a preacher is James S.

Stewart of Edinburgh. In his Warrack Lectures he says:

> My second plea is for a due observance of the Christian Year.
> . . . The great landmarks of the Christian Year—Advent, Christmas,
> Lent, Good Friday, Easter, Whitsunday, Trinity—set us our course,
> and suggest our basic themes. They compel us to keep close to the
> fundamental doctrines of our faith. They summon us back from the
> bypaths where we might be prone to linger, to the great highway of
> redemption. They ensure that in our preaching we shall constantly
> be returning to those mighty acts of God which the church exists to
> declare.[2]

Is Stewart able to practice effectively what he preaches? This is
how Professor Horton Davies of Princeton University characterizes
Stewart's preaching:

> So much of modern preaching is hesitant where Stewart is
> assured, so vague where Stewart is definite, moralistic where
> Stewart announces good news (the gift of Christ and not what *we
> have to give up* to be Christians). So much modern preaching is
> merely further diagnosis of the dreary political and social crisis,
> where Stewart proclaims the Incarnation, the Cross, the Resurrec-
> tion and the Second Coming of Christ, to be the single all-important
> cosmic crisis, by whom God judges, forgives, renews, and raises
> hope in man. Stewart is direct where others are devious, exhilarating
> where others are dull.[3]

This is a faithful description of the preaching of one who knows
the kerygma and who is conscious, so very conscious, of the
Christian Year and its implications for preaching.

Observe now how the different emphases in this early preaching
are preserved in the Christian Year. Within the bounds of the seven
major seasons, every great note of the kerygma is called forth.

Advent

The Christian Year begins with the Advent season, the Sunday
nearest November 30. As stated earlier, Advent connotes "arrival,"
or "coming." It also suggests that which is yet to come. Advent rejoices in the past, in the present, and in the future. It proclaims the

salvation that was promised in the past, that is realized in the present, and the completion of which is anticipated in the future. Christ came; the prophets had greeted his presence from afar. He came in the incarnation; the incarnation continues in and through the church. He will come as judge to complete his redeeming work.

Another note that the preacher should sound in his preaching during the Advent season has to do with time. In and through Advent, time itself is redeemed. Time is no longer a matter of tomorrows, creeping on in petty pace, the todays dropping off into a bottomless abyss to make room for more tomorrows that will likewise be lost in some limbo of the past. That would, indeed, be "a tale told by an idiot, full of sound and fury, signifying nothing."

But such is not the case. Through the great truths of Advent, time becomes a friend, a treasure house that has on deposit the everlasting past and the very present future. These deposits are for use in the eternal now, and the child of God makes his own deposits and has his own withdrawal rights. The Christ who is the same yesterday, today, and forever guarantees the account. Neither things present nor things to come can separate the disciple from his Master who redeems time. Try that doctrine on for size against the meaninglessness of existence that is the current style!

Advent sounds the note of "the gospel of the blessed God" who created and continues creation, who reigned, reigns, and shall reign until he has put all enemies under his feet. Dr. William Temple wrote: "While we deliberate, He reigns; when we decide wisely, He reigns; when we decide foolishly, He reigns; when we serve humbly and loyally, He reigns; when we serve Him self-assertively, He reigns; when we rebel and seek to withhold our service, He reigns—the Alpha and the Omega, which is, and which was, and which is to come, the Almighty." [4] That is Advent's authentic note, a note prevalent in the preaching of the apostles but seldom heard today. No wonder the genuine cry and prayer of his followers for centuries has been, "Come, Lord Jesus!"

It is said that on the evening preceding August 1 in 1830, the slaves in the West Indian colonies did not sleep. It was the night before the day of their promised freedom. They assembled in their places of worship by the tens of thousands. Some of their numbers were sent to the hills to watch for the first streaks of dawn that would announce the day of their liberation. Those on the hill would, by prearranged signals, announce to their brethren in the valleys below that they were no longer chattels. The sun was coming and its beams announced that they were children of freedom.

The coming of the Son of God does that. "O come, O come, Immanuel! and ransom captive Israel!" That is Advent. What a theme for preaching!

Use that theme for the four Sundays of Advent, the four Sundays with the different emphases: creation, the Bible, the prophets, and the Forerunner. The listing of a few sermon titles will indicate something of the need for and significance of such preaching:

History: His Story
God Keeps His Appointments
God's Purpose in Christmas
Advent Is a Long Christmas
    Eve
The Difference His Coming
    Makes

Communication, God's Problem, Too
God's Preparation and Ours
Gangway, Gangway for De Lawd God Jehovah
Our Eternal Contemporary
How the Word Gets Through

With such themes, there need be no lack of relevance, freshness, and authority for a minister's preaching program, no matter how long he preaches to the same congregation.

Christmastide

Christmastide has one or two Sundays, depending upon the position of Christmas Day in the week. The emphasis of Advent is upon *preparation*; the emphasis of Christmas is upon *receiving*. The message of the first-century preachers proclaimed that what the prophets had seen from afar had now come to pass. This event came about by "the determinate counsel and foreknowledge of God." It was man's privilege and responsibility to be receptive to God's act in sending Christ. This Christ was descended from David; he came in the flesh and dwelt among us.

Leonard Griffith tells a delightful story about a group of English schoolchildren constructing a manger scene in one corner of their classroom. They built the barn and covered the floor with hay. The figures of Mary, Joseph, the shepherds, the Wise Men, and the animals were all facing the cradle. A tiny doll represented the baby Jesus. The children were excited, but one little fellow seemed troubled. He returned again and again to the corner of the room to study the manger scene. Finally, the teacher asked if something was wrong. Revealing wisdom typical of a child's ability to confound the wise, he said, "What I'd like to know is—where does God fit in?" [5]

It is an important question. It needs to be asked not only of the extreme commercialization of the season by business interests; it needs to be asked and clearly answered in relation to many of our "religious" customs and celebrations. "Where does God fit in?" To answer the question is a basic responsibility of preaching in Christmastide. If the responsibility is to be worthily discharged, the preaching will need to be planned and purposeful.

If the question asked by the child is answered truthfully, it will have to be answered in the light of the Old Testament teaching, in the light of the kerygma. To receive the Christ of Christmas is to receive the Messiah whom the prophets foretold. It is essential that we receive a *whole* Christ, not just Bethlehem's babe; it is essential to receive the man of Galilee who went about doing good; it is necessary to receive the crucified and reigning Saviour, the resurrected and reigning Lord, the ascended Christ, the one who is to be the judge of the "quick and the dead."

Preaching must be related to man's plight. Indeed, it is at this point that such preaching as Peter's and Paul's is so entirely relevant. How could it be otherwise with a proclamation that shows God in the midst of daily life—especially daily life at Christmas time which is so alien to all that the celebration stands for.

Look at titles used for relevant sermons that proclaim the great truths of the season:

God Invades the World
Operation Christmas
Christmas Expectations

Home for Christmas
A White Christmas—With What?

God Has Priority	The Hope of Christmas
Life Is a Bethlehem Inn	The Christmas Hymn
Serving an Adult Christ	The Crown Rights of the Re-
He Came Too Soon, Did He?	deemer

In Aldous Huxley's *The Genius and the Goddess,* John Rivers goes to the door with a friend and, opening the door, cautions him to drive carefully since it is the Saviour's birthday in a Christian country and nearly everyone is drunk.

Contrast that with the great gospel truths:

The Word became flesh and dwelt among us (John 1:14,RSV).
Who, though he was in the form of God, did not count equality with God a thing to be grasped, but emptied himself, taking the form of a servant, being born in the likeness of men (Phil. 2:6–7,RSV).
I bring you good news of great joy which will come to all the people; for to you is born this day in the city of David a Savior (Luke 2:10–11,RSV).

Again, for the child's question to be answered truthfully, the preacher must answer it in terms of the God-Man, Immanuel (God with us). For, just as man's highest end is to serve God, so God's greatest concern as revealed in the Christian truth is to seek, to find, and to redeem man.

Through this fact, that God has become man, time and human life are changed. Not to the extent that he has ceased to be himself, the Eternal Word of God himself, with all his splendor and unimaginable bliss. But he has really become man. And now this world and its destiny concern him. Now it is not only his work, but a part of his very self. Now he no longer watches its course as a spectator; he himself is now within it. What is expected of us is now expected of him; our lot now falls upon him, our earthly joy as well as the wretchedness that is proper for us. Now we no longer need to seek him in the endless heavens, where our spirits and our hearts get lost. Now he himself is on our very earth, where he is no better off than we and where he receives no special privileges, but our very fate: hunger, weariness, enmity, mortal terror and wretched death. That the infinity of God should take upon itself the human narrowness, that bliss should accept the mortal sorrow of the earth, that life should take on death—this is the most unlikely truth. But only this—the obscure light of faith—makes our nights bright, only this makes them holy. God has come. He is there in the world.[6]

The tense of some of those verbs may disturb us, but the biblical thrust is unmistakable. It is this biblical orientation that was so evident in the preaching of Peter and Paul; it is the Christian Year that will not let us forget nor fail to observe it.

Epiphany

Epiphany means manifestation, uncovering, revealing. The events in the life of Christ connected with the season are the coming of the Wise Men, the baptism, and the first miracle at Cana. As Advent accentuates preparation and Christmas emphasizes reception, so Epiphany affirms searching, pilgrimage, and manifestation. In Christmas we celebrate God's gift to man. In Epiphany we celebrate man's gifts to God—his searching, his love, his talents, his gold, frankincense, and myrrh.

The initiative is still with God, yet there is a matter of pilgrimage that is left to man. Stars must be followed; prodigals must repent, come to themselves, and return to their father's house. Men go to Christ who came to men, and as they go, they bear gifts. Epiphany, then, is the time for evangelism and missions. The promise goes out even to those who are afar off, even to as many as the Lord God shall call. In reality, this is where it all begins. The manifestation "to the Gentiles" is the manifestation of God, and it is God who is manifested.

Men do not establish the kingdom; only God is mighty enough for that. When men get into the act, they get in by invitation only. All kingdom building is theologically oriented. So far as social, economic, and political programs are concerned, the man of God "couldn't care less." But the man of God does care, and he cares passionately, about the will, the purpose, and the love of God. It is out of this manifestation of God—his loving concern for his children —that the man of God becomes concerned about these issues. Therefore, it is fitting that the preacher take note of two important days in the church calendar during February—Race Relations Sunday and Brotherhood Sunday.

The parables of the kingdom are especially appropriate for a preaching program during this season. From the beginning, it was the task of the followers of Jesus to live in the hope of, and to give themselves unreservedly to, the control of God in kingdom building. The kerygma declared that Christ had been exalted at the right hand of God, that God had "made him Lord and Christ." He had been rejected by the builders, but God had made him "the head of the corner." Epiphany says it loud and clear: the applying of the gospel to every area of man's life is not an elective but a required course.

There is one additional note that needs to be sounded in preaching during this season; that note has to do with methods and programs. It must be remembered that it is God who is to be manifested. The power and the glory are his, not man's. Methods, techniques, and programs have to be in keeping with God, his interests, his concerns, and his Spirit. It is possible to do the work of God in a way that dishonors God. Christ refused to accept the "kingdoms of this world" if doing so required him to accept them at the hands of evil. The ends never justify the means; the means will always modify the ends. Our "hows" have to be theologically oriented no less than our "whats." Epiphany says that our methods have to undergo regeneration. There are some methods that man cannot use even for the purpose of saving his brother, for such methods would dishonor the Father. Ultimately, no method that dishonors the Father can honor the brother. It is God's Word and kingdom that must be our guide in all the concerns and hurts of life.[7]

Lent

Lent is a season of preparation for the climax of the Christian Year and of Christian faith—the resurrection. Preparation through investigation, self-examination, self-denial, and true repentance is not to the end that the worshiper might become worthy of celebrating the season of our Lord's resurrection. That is and always will be impossible. Rather, the preparation is to the end that the worshiper may recognize and be receptive to God's mighty act. Lent and the disciplines suggested by it are never for their own sakes. Lent looks beyond itself; it has significance only in the light of Easter. Lent is to the resurrection as repentance is to salvation.

In his preaching during this season the minister needs to remember that there is no other season in the Christian Year that seems as incongruous to modern man as this period of discipline, sacrifice, and penitence. Today is not noted for its discipline or restraint. Instead, it is a time of "freedom" and demonstrations, violent and nonviolent. The times detest controls and restraints of any kind. This is true of both interior and exterior regulations. If there is a custom, break it; if there are laws, unless they seem good to the individual, either break those laws or exert pressures to change them.

From another point of view Lent seems out of place in the modern world. One of the season's major notes is that of aloneness. It calls upon the worshiper to come into the "desert" experiences, to isolate himself from the crowd. Yet, deep within, man has never been more alone than in the twentieth century. He is one of the "lonely crowd"; he is in the midst of people but he is not one of the people. Nothing shows this more clearly than notes left by the increasing number of those who commit suicide. To tell modern man that he needs to experience aloneness—to tell him that the churches in their observance of Lent offer this to him—is to offer modern man what he already has too much of!

This sense of loneliness is not limited only to the nonbeliever; the disciples know the gnawing hunger no less, although from a different point of view. Righteousness is like dope: the more the patient partakes of it, the greater his craving for it.

The believer may recognize the symptoms for what they really are. He may say with the psalmist, "As the hart panteth after the water brooks, so panteth my soul after thee, O God" (42:1). The nonbeliever may not recognize the symptoms, and if he did, he would not admit it. Still, there is incompleteness. Sermon titles such as these should be helpful: "The Rewards of Aloneness," "The Solace of Solitude," "The Conquest of Inner Space," "Prepare to Meet Thy God on a Cross."

In the celebration of Lent the cross is always present, like the pillar of cloud by day and of fire by night. In his program of preaching, the minister can never get very far from the verse, "Take up thy cross and follow me." Jane McKay Lanning sounded the note in her little poem "Lent."

> To search our souls,
> To meditate,
> Will not suffice for Lent.
>
> To share the cross,
> To sacrifice,
> These are the things
> God meant.[8]

There are certain days within the season of Lent which a minister needs to magnify for the spiritual enrichment of his people. These are Palm Sunday, the Sunday before Easter; Maundy Thursday, the Thursday of Holy Week; and Good Friday, the Friday before Easter.

Most churches recognize Palm Sunday and commemorate the triumphal entry of Jesus into Jerusalem. On that day common people welcomed him with glad shouts of praise, garments stripped from their quivering bodies, palm branches waved with enthusiasm. It was a day worthy of remembrance.

Maundy Thursday comes from the Latin word for mandate. It refers to Christ's new commandment "that ye love one another." The words were given on Thursday evening before the crucifixion. Since, according to our time keeping, it is the anniversary of the first observance of the Lord's Supper, the night offers the finest opportunity of the year for the observance of the beloved event. Through memories, associations, treasured Scripture verses, greatly loved hymns and poetry, and strong preaching that is tender, it can be a blessed event. It is as though the bread and the cup are received from the very hands of the Saviour himself as we hear the words, "This do in remembrance of me."

There are indications that Good Friday may have originally been called "God's Friday." It is often observed in a three-hour service at midday; frequently it is a community service. The long service is broken at regular points as the seven words spoken by Jesus from the cross are emphasized. Sometimes no formal service is held and members of the churches are invited to come for quiet meditation during the three-hour period. Through carefully planned services, thoughtful teaching, and warmhearted preaching, the impact of Hester H. Cholmondeley may be experienced:

> Still as of old
> Men by themselves are priced—
> For thirty pieces Judas sold
> Himself, not Christ.[9]

Eastertide

Easter was the first great event to be celebrated by the early churches. The instinct of the churches was unerring. It is difficult to see how any part of the calendar would have meaning apart from Easter. Three-fourths of the Christian calendar is determined by the date of Easter. Old John Keble said of Easter: "Thou art the sun of other days,/They shine by giving back thy rays."

Easter Sunday gives opportunity for celebrating the resurrection of Jesus Christ; Eastertide gives the churches opportunity to proclaim the meaning and significance of the resurrection for the church. Easter Sunday is inadequate for all the trumpet blasts that need to be heard; Eastertide takes cognizance of this fact. Throughout the fifty days leading up to Pentecost the churches are encouraged to sound such notes as these:

God's Victory over Sin and Death
Christ's Lordship on Earth and in Heaven

The Roots of a Vital Faith
The Quality, Content, and Extent of Eternal Life over Mortality

Central Certainties for Uncer- The Significance of Life Lived
   tain Times   Out in the Light of the Resur-
The Conquest of Outer Space   rection

When the preacher proclaims such great themes faithfully and
effectively, there is no anticlimactic feeling in the church such as is
often experienced following Easter Sunday. With such a program of
proclamation, Easter Sunday is no longer a peak from which the
individual and church can go only downward. With a worthy plan
and program, the mighty spiritual stream that reached its crest on
Easter continues on its full and purposeful way through ascension to
Pentecost. There it is joined by the mighty inflowing of the Holy
Spirit, and the church of the living God is launched.

There is another reason for the season of Eastertide and not limit-
ing the celebration just to Easter Sunday. The faithful minister
often faces a dilemma on that Sunday. That mighty day is a time
for trumpet blasts, for great affirmations, the great truths of the
kerygma. On this day of days it is "not his to reason why," it is his
to "proclaim and declare!" Yet, every intelligent minister knows that
if he hopes to reach the educated mind of today, he has to somehow "outthink" those minds—minds that are limited to scientific
horizons. Everything about that scientific mind is against the truths
of the resurrection.

Although Easter Sunday is not the time for it, analysis and
apologetics cannot be left out of a helpful preaching program. Within the time limit of Eastertide, "The Great Fifty Days," the good
minister of Jesus Christ can enter into dialogue with his hearers
about the meaning and significance of the resurrection. He can say
to them, "Come, let us reason together." He can show that the
death of Jesus did not take God by surprise, nor did it defeat God's
plan and purpose. While God did not save his Son from the cross,
he did do something greater—he saved his Son and us by the cross.
Of that the resurrection and resulting church are proof.

Within the season of Eastertide and on the border of Pentecost
comes Ascensiontide. The early preachers declared that Jesus had
been exalted at the right hand of God, and that he had been
"ordained of God to be Judge of quick and dead." The modern-day

preacher cannot afford to allow the space age to take away his Lord. And the minister cannot go stumbling about, giving the impression that he does not know where they have laid his Lord. There is no better time to come to terms with this problem than at the Ascension season. Through careful attention to semantic principles, through careful communion with the kerygma truths, the preacher can effectively proclaim that Christ is Lord of the universe.

Pentecost

Pentecost indicates fifty. The event comes fifty days after the Passover. For the Jews it marked the celebration of the giving of the Law and the Feast of Weeks. For the followers of Christ it meant the fulfilment of the promise God made through the prophet Joel that God would pour out his Spirit upon all flesh. In the Ascension, Christ left his disciples to return to the Father. In the coming of the Holy Spirit, Christ returned in a new form never to leave them again. The church now became his body; through the church he does his work. Pentecost is emphasized as the birthday of the church; in that celebration let us not forget the Holy Spirit, who was responsible for the birth.

The kerygma always emphasized the need for repentance. Through repentance, forgiveness is offered; the Holy Spirit is a gift to all who will receive him. In some way, then, preaching during Pentecost takes on the characteristics of preaching in Advent. There a plea is made that we make room for the Christ, that he be received hospitably. In Pentecost the plea is made that we "resist not the Holy Spirit."

Trinity Sunday is the Sunday after Pentecost Sunday. This is the most appropriate time for the preacher to proclaim this great doctrine. And it is not an easy doctrine to proclaim. Each minister will have to search his own mind and heart and library for all the assistance available. Leonard Griffith has a helpful sermon in which he sees God the Father as "God above and beyond us," God the Son as "God with us," and God the Holy Spirit as "God within us." It is a helpful vehicle. St. Francis found help in his private devotion by repeating and meditating upon the doxology: "Glory be to the

Father, and to the Son, and to the Holy Ghost; As it was in the beginning, is now, and ever shall be, world without end. Amen."

Every individual, group, and institution is motivated by some spirit. It may be the spirit of selfishness and greed, of lust and pride, of race, creed, or class. Pentecost is the time to declare for the Spirit of God. The analogy has been drawn that if a man had the spirit of Shakespeare, he could write like Shakespeare; if he had the spirit of Einstein, he could understand the intricacies of science and mathematics as Einstein understood them. When one has the Spirit of God, he can do the works of God.

This is the practical mysticism that the people of God need. Man is created in the image of God; he has great potential for light and heat and power. The missing ingredient is the flame of the Holy Spirit.

Kingdomtide

With Kingdomtide the entire force of the kerygmatic preaching is brought to bear upon man's daily life and human relationships. Certain important occasions and days in this season add to the appropriateness of the emphasis: Labor Day Sunday, Reformation Sunday, Temperance Sunday, Back to School Sunday, World Communion Sunday, World Peace Sunday, World Order Sunday, Community Fund, Thanksgiving.

It is easier for a preacher to emphasize such causes if the days are a part of his calendar; if it is understood that other ministers and churches are sounding the same themes; if newspapers, magazines, church periodicals, radio, and television are doing their part to prepare the people for proclamation upon such issues. Kingdomtide, along with Epiphany, says that nothing worthy of concern to man should be alien to the gospel of Christ.

By joining the kerygma and the Christian Year, every major emphasis in the life and ministry of Christ, every note and accent of the Christian gospel will find their places in a minister's preaching program.

DECEMBER, YEAR

	Event	A.M.	P.M.	Wed.

1st Week in Adv.	Advent, 1st Sunday
	
	WMU Week of Prayer for Foreign Missions B
		————————(Sun. date)
		Scripture Lessons:
		  Gen. 1:26-31
		  Col. 1:12-22
		Text: 2 Cor. 5:17
		Title: "Gangway for the Lord God Jehovah"
		God creates: then and now.
			————————(Sun. date)
			Scripture Lessons:
			  Isa. 42:1-4
			  Matt. 27:11-14
			Text: Matt. 27:14
			Title: "No Ear May Hear His Coming"
			"He never said a mumlin' word."
				————————(Sun. date)
				Scripture:
				  Luke 11:1-13
				Text: Job 21:15
				Title: "Prayer and World Missions"
				
				(Women in charge)

2nd Week in Adv.	Advent, 2nd Sunday
	
	Training Union "M" Night B
		Scripture Lessons:
		  Jer. 33:14-16
		  Rom. 15:4-13
		Text: Luke 24:27
		Title: "Great Expectations"
		All the Scriptures looked forward to his coming.
			Scripture Lesson:
			  Rom. 10:3-18
			Text: Rom. 3:10
			Title: "But In This World of Sin"
			"He came too soon, this Christ of peace." (Maxwell Anderson)
				Scripture:
				  1 John 3:1-11
				Title: "Christ in Art"
				
				Lessons from art in the great paintings on the Nativity

3rd Week in Adv.	Advent, 3rd Sunday
	
	Universal Bible Sunday
		Scripture Lessons:
		  Isa. 52:7-10
		  1 Cor. 4:1-5
		Text: Isa. 21:11
		Title: "Watchman, What of the Night"
		"God speaks and there's hanging to be done.
			Scripture Lesson:
			  John 1:11-13
			Text: John 1:12
			Title: "Where Meek Souls Will Receive Him"
			
			A time for hospitality
				Scripture:
				  1 Cor. 13
				Title: "Christ in Music and Poetry"
				
				The season reminds us of our debt to musicians and poets.

4th Week in Adv.	Advent, 4th Sunday
	
	Convention-wide Carol Sing in the B Churches Christmas Day
		Scripture Lessons:
		  Isa: 40:1-11
		  Luke 3:1-16a
		Text: Luke 3:4
		Title: "Ready for His Coming?"
		Preparation is essential to all great experiences.
			Scripture Lesson:
			  John 14:15-23
			Text: John 14:23
			Title: "The Dear Christ Enters In"
			"Who, when, where, how?
				Scripture:
				  Luke 2:1-20
				Title: "Christ in Story and Scripture"

1st Sun. of Christmas	Christmastide
	
	Student Night at Christmas B
	
	Student Recognition M
		Scripture Lessons:
		  Zech. 2:10-13
		  John 1:1-18
		Text: John 1:1
		Title: "Communication—God's Problem, Too"
			Student Night At Christmas
			
			(Students in charge of service)
				Scripture:
				  Psalm 90
				Texts: Ezek. 44:2, Rev. 3:8, 20
				Title: "Please Close the Door —Please Open the Door"

6

Preaching Through
the Bible

(PLAN II)

Judy Holliday once starred in a play written by Goodman Ace. After her performance the critics were extremely critical of the material. Miss Holliday wrote an apologetic letter to the author, saying that she felt the critics were unjust, for she regarded the material as excellent. She concluded: "The fault, I am sorry to say, lay with the performance. I just didn't go that extra step to master it." [1]

In planning his preaching program, a minister has to make up his mind about the Bible. Is the material good or bad? When the "play" fails, is it due to the material or to the weak performance of the material? Does he need new and different material or does the material only require that "extra step to master it"?

The second preaching plan proceeds on the latter assumption— that there is nothing wrong with the material. This plan is designated by the accurate, if unromantic name, "Preaching Through the Bible." The idea is to begin preaching in Genesis and to move straight through to Revelation, no matter how long the journey may take. The plan may be so organized that the material will be covered in one year, or it may be so planned that it will take fifteen years to complete the journey.

The choice will have to be made whether each of the weekly services will be included in the plan, or whether just one or two of these services will be included. Any combination may be used, and used effectively.

If the very idea of the plan, beginning with the first book in the

Bible and preaching straight through to the last book, seems to be a
formidable one (and it doubtless will seem so to the man who has
never followed such a procedure), remember that some of the most
successful ministers are enthusiastic in their use of it. The word
"success" may raise more questions than it settles. Yet, while a "successful church" may be hard to define, it is not difficult to recognize
when it is seen. It surely is not a matter of size alone; small churches
may be successful, while large churches may be unsuccessful, or
vice versa. Ministers of both use the plan.

Consider a specific example. A man is minister of a large and
"successful" metropolitan church; he is active in his denomination on
the local, state, national, and international levels. His radio ministry
reaches millions of listeners at home and overseas every week. He
says:

I highly recommend the plan. We need to preach the Bible, not
just sermons from or about the Bible! There is a dearth of Bible-
centered preaching today. We need more expository preaching.
The Bible is a logical book which outlines itself if we permit it to
do so, and its message is applicable to the needs of this age and
every age.

I have followed the plan without any sense of being in a strait-
jacket. I feel free to drop it when needs arise to do some other
type of preaching, but I always come back to it. It has resulted in
our people bringing their Bibles to the services and following the
text as I preach. Sometimes I use one verse, at other times I use a
paragraph, a chapter, a character, or in some cases an entire book
for one sermon. I let the need determine the plan. It has been of
interest to me through the years to note that as I have preached
through the Bible, situations would arise in which the very passage
coming up would be the one with a message our people needed at
that time. The plan provides continuity and variety; it enables the
preacher to touch on social and human needs, not as a "hobby,"
but as the unfolding word of God.[2]

Advantages

One obvious point in favor of such a plan is the place of honor that
it gives to the Word of God. The preacher who conscientiously
follows this plan shows that he *respects the entire Bible*. He is no

respecter of certain passages of Scripture. This does not mean that
he will spend an equal amount of time with each book, or each
part of any one book. It does mean that the entire Bible, "warts and
all," will be given careful attention in the preaching program.

Unless Protestants have gone a long sea mile from their early
biblical teaching and their Reformation heritage, such a position
has distinct advantages. Ezekiel's words are to the point: "The word
of the Lord came unto me, saying, Son of man, prophesy against the
prophets of Israel that prophesy, and say thou unto them that
prophesy out of their own hearts, Hear ye the word of the Lord"
(13:1-2).

It is no secret that a man may preach interesting, stimulating,
relevant, dynamic sermons that have little to do with the Bible.
Doubt it? It has often been done.

A second point in favor of such a preaching program rests on
perspective. For a long time much was made of the position that the
Bible is not a Book so much as it is a library of books. The point, of
course, is well taken. There are sixty-six books within the covers of
one Book. These books were written by many different individuals
over a thousand years in time, and with different, immediate goals
in mind.

But this viewpoint can be misleading. This "Bible library" is more
different from than it is similar to a public library—different in
motive and purpose. Further, the selection and relationship between the books that make up the "Bible library" are not the same
as those that make up the public library. In the public library it is
possible to read many books with little or no thought of any relationship between the books. You may read books without your
understanding being penalized for not having read other books. The
situation is not so simple with the books of the Bible.

No one understands the New Testament with any degree of
thoroughness without first understanding something of the Old
Testament. The biblical books of history and poetry have to be read
and understood in the light of the books of law, and vice versa.
Marcion of the second century, Thomas Jefferson of the seventeenth
and Abraham Lincoln of the nineteenth centuries were not very

clear about this, but the preacher should be clear. R. W. Barbour was clear in his understanding of the issue when he wrote:

He who has not felt what *sin* is in the Old Testament knows little of what *grace* is in the New. He who has not trembled with Moses, and wept with David, and wondered in Isaiah, will rejoice little in Matthew, rest little in John. He who has not suffered under the Law will scarcely hear the glad sound of the gospel. He who has not been awakened under the mountain will be little delighted with the cross.[3]

The helpful preacher will preach each sermon, whatever the source of his particular text, in the light of the teachings of the entire Bible. The best commentary on any part of the Bible is the rest of the Bible. This is not to appeal for proof-text methods; it is to say that the Bible is its best interpreter. It is this that is meant by *perspective* in preaching. The minister who preaches through the Bible has perspective; at least, he has the equipment for securing a valid perspective. And without perspective, a man's preaching may be "eager and brave," but it will not be mature and abiding. Browning knew this when he said that if we draw a circle premature, heedless of far gain, greedy only for quick returns of profit, the bargain is bad. And Edna St. Vincent Millay knew it when she wrote:

If you live in the street called, *Now*, in a house called *Here*—
If you live at Number Here North Now Street, let us say,
Then immediate things, discomfort, sorrow, it is clear,
Are of first importance; you could feel no other way.
But if you pitch your tent each evening nearer the town
Of your true desire, and glimpse its gates less far,
Then you lay you down on nettles, you lay you down
With vipers, and you scarcely notice where you are.
The world is not relinquished; but the world assumes
Its proper place in perspective.[4]

Preaching that is within the context of the full biblical revelation, preaching that is patient and content to wait for worthy fruit, this is the outgrowth of following a plan of preaching that takes a man straight through the Bible.

Discipline

Consider a third point: Such a preaching plan *disciplines the preacher*. It will make him a constant student. He does not search week after independent week for tempting lures to cast before the mental and emotional striking range of his people, while the next week he is out looking for more tantalizing tackle. Instead, he consistently provides a diet that is nourishing. Jesus said that he would teach his followers to be fishers of men. He did not mean that he would teach them to be tricksters but that he would teach them now to dispense the bread of life, and in the filling of hungry hearts, his followers would find their success.

It is easy for a man to base his preaching program on reactions, his preaching from week to week being determined by passing events and circumstances. Long ago Demosthenes scolded his fellow Athenians for acting so in war. His words are equally apropos for many a minister's preaching program. The Greek orator wrote:

Shame on you Athenians, for not wishing to understand that one must not allow oneself to be at the command of events, but must forestall them. You move against Philip like a barbarian when he wrestles. If you hear Philip has attacked in Cheronese, you run there. If he is at Thermopylae, you run there. If he turns aside, you follow him, to the right, to the left, as if you are acting on his orders. Never a fixed plan. You wait for bad news before you act.[5]

In the fourth place, this plan is valuable for the *preacher's own spiritual enrichment*. That is important. Someone reported on going to a small restaurant and finding the door locked and a card hanging from the knob which read: "Out for lunch, back in an hour." The man evidently knew the quality of his own food, and how he reacted to that knowledge should have been significant for his would-be customers. The preacher should partake of the food that he feeds to his people and his own soul should be nourished thereby.

There is much to be said for a man spending his life in a careful study of the Scriptures. To follow a preaching plan that *requires* such discipline is no small consideration.

Some years ago a friend began his ministry in a church just off the campus of a world-renowned university. Many members of the faculty were members of his church. After the first sermon, a member of the faculty came and corrected the preacher on something he had said in his sermon. Then the professor added: "Dr. Blank, you will have to remember that no matter what you preach about in this pulpit, there will be someone in the audience who knows more about the subject than you do." It ain't necessarily so! If a preacher spends his life in a careful, scholarly, devotional study of the Scriptures, he should know more about those Scriptures from the standpoint of proclamation than any person who may be in his audience. From the standpoint of mediating the truths of God to his own people, he should be like Saul of old, head and shoulders above anyone else in the crowd.

Variety

In the fifth place, this plan offers *freshness and variety*. Early in his life, George Bernard Shaw gave up the job of being drama critic for a London weekly paper. In explaining his action, Shaw said that his job was like fighting a windmill. "I hardly have time to stagger to my feet from the knockdown blow of one sail, when the next one strikes me down."

The pastor knows about that. In writing of the Bible as a perennial source of freshness and variety in contrast to any other preaching source, Luccock said: "But a congregation gets to know our witness on contemporary social and economic and intellectual questions. Man cannot live on an exclusive diet of the United Nations or atomic control. By the time you give your seventh sermon of the season on these things, the congregation gets the general idea of your stand on these issues." [6] The Bible is a well of fresh water springing up from week to week.

Just after he had preached his fourth sermon, the young preacher George Johnstone Jeffrey made his way to a trusted older minister. The present was discouraging and the future was black for young Jeffrey. After preaching four sermons, he had run out of something to preach; his well was dry. The thought of standing before the same congregation Sunday after Sunday, year after year, was nothing short of stark tragedy. The older minister heard him out and then spoke three words that Jeffrey never forgot. He said, "The manna falls." It does; the manna falls. And the manna falls nowhere with such freshness and variety as if does on the plains of the Scriptures, when a man cultivates those fields as the source of his preaching year in and year out.

Consider a sixth advantage in preaching through the Bible: The plan will *embrace the whole range of revelation.* Much was made in chapter 5 of this point. The plan of preaching through the Bible has the same advantage although it approaches the subject in a different way. No minister is adequate to perform the task on his own. He has to say with Paul, we know in part and we prophesy in part. But the preacher who takes the entire Bible as his guide will declare the whole counsel of God.

After a strong and emphatic sermon on a great biblical doctrine, one of the older members of the church said to the preacher: "Young man, you are mighty inexperienced for such preaching." The young minister, with commendable courage and questionable diplomacy answered: "Madam, I represent eternity!" Good! He does and he can by a careful, diligent, continuous proclamation of the whole Word of God.

It is doubtful that any minister, young or old, is fully qualified to choose between the different parts of the total revelation of God for his people as if to say to them: "This you need; this you do not need. This I declare to you; but, this I withhold from you." No, it were better that he seek earnestly to declare the whole counsel of God, and this he will do if he preaches through the Bible.

In seeking to declare the full revelation of God, a man will be dispensing strong meat. There will be times when the doctrine will have to be dispensed in the form of milk. However, it may be that the danger faced by the average minister is not that he will feed his people a diet that is too strong for them, but rather that the needs of the people will call for a stronger diet than he is willing or able to give them.

Years ago, Joseph Noyes was minister of the First Church of New Haven. It was the home of the newly transplanted Yale College.

Members of the college administration, faculty, and student body were in constant attendance at the church. Indeed, the students were required to attend on pain of having to pay a penalty of twenty shillings for each absence. President Clap was disturbed about the quality of the preaching and went to talk to his pastor about it. Pastor Noyes replied: "You do not know what ignorant people I have to preach to." "Yes, I do," responded President Clap, "and I know that as long as you preach to them this way they will remain ignorant."

There is another observation to be made about preaching through the Bible: It will make way for the *proper observance of special days.* This is one of the first objections that is voiced of the plan. It is felt that if the minister has bound himself to a plan that requires him to plow straight through the Bible, he will find himself in the Desert of Sinai with Moses when he should be on pilgrimage to Jerusalem with the Wise Men; or he will be fighting the wars with the judges when he should be going with the disciples to the empty tomb. But in actual fact, the minister has no insolvable problem here.

In the first place, the plan is always servant, not master, of the preacher. The plan was made for preaching, not preaching for the plan. It is fitting and proper for a preacher to leave any preaching plan for any special day, provided his people can be better served by his doing so. If he leaves the plan for a special day, he can return to the plan after the celebration of that day.

There is still another word to be said. Men who have used the plan over the years bear witness that such difficulties are more apparent than real. These men affirm that in actual practice the times are few, and these have wide spaces between them, when a man needs to leave the plan. Again and again, as some deserving emphasis in the calendar comes upon the horizon, the preacher will see that it can be dealt with legitimately, creatively, and helpfully by staying on the scriptural trail that he has been following.

At this point hark back to the former discussion on the growth and development of New Testament events and celebrations from the Old Testament heritage, and remember that while the Bible is a library of many books, it is also one Book made up of many volumes. No plea is made for forcing the Scriptures to say what they were not meant to say. The preacher must always be on his guard against reading into the Scripture passages what the writer would be amazed to find there! Let it be remembered, however, that it is equally bad to ignore sources and origins. The lines of communication between different passages of Scripture, as well as between certain passages of Scripture and events to be celebrated, are often much closer than a superficial reading and study indicate.

Let this fact be noted also: The plan of preaching through the Bible offers opportunity for abundant variety in *types and forms of preaching.* If preaching forms are thought of in traditional terms—expository, textual, and topical—the plan obviously yields itself to such treatment. In beginning the plan, it would be wise to preach a sermon or a brief series of sermons on the Bible as a whole. Such titles as "The Bible Speaks to Our Day," "How to Read the Bible," or "Dangers in Reading the Bible" are good openers. Sections of the Bible, such as law, history, poetry, or the gospels, may be dealt with in sermons. Great ideas of the Bible may be used as the basis for sermons: What Is Man? What Is the Meaning of Life? Why Are We Here? Where Are We Going? What Is the Meaning of Death? Such themes may rely upon single texts or upon the entire Bible.

In recent years there has been a movement toward a more solid biblical basis for preaching. One way the movement has manifested itself is in using larger blocks of Scripture. This movement is indicated by Dwight E. Stevenson's two fine books, *Preaching on the Books of the Old Testament* and *Preaching on the Books of the New Testament.* My book, *The Life and Letters of Paul,* gives a book sermon on each of Paul's letters. Sections of Scripture (more or less than a chapter) or the whole chapter make good preaching units. "Golden Chapters" in the Bible have long been a favorite source of preaching. Preaching from Bible paragraphs has probably been the most popular unit of Scripture. The single sentence, verse, phrase, clause, and word have all been effectively used. One of the most helpful books for preaching on these various divisions of Scripture is *A Guide to Biblical Preaching,* by Chalmer E. Faw.

In his Lyman Beecher Lectures, published under the title *The*

Modern Use of the Bible, Fosdick said there were four ways to know the Bible: you could know it through its beauty spots, its individual books, its characters, and its ideas. There are other rich veins of preaching ore, such as rivers of the Bible, mountains of the Bible, seas of the Bible, flowers and birds of the Bible, (Jesus preached effectively on these last two), the trees of the Bible, the nights of the Bible, the dawns of the Bible. These are enough to suggest something of the wide variety of forms and types of preaching a man may use in his plan of preaching through the Bible.

How to Do It

By taking a single book of the Bible and pointing out a few of the preaching opportunities it offers, it will be easy to see how a minister can develop his plan of preaching through the Bible. No effort will be made to designate what materials would be most fitting for the different services.

As stated earlier, it would be wise to begin the program by preaching one or more sermons on the Bible as a whole. Each book needs to be seen in the light of the entire Bible. The sermons on the Bible as a whole would be followed by one or more sermons on the particular book—Genesis, for example. Faw suggests five types of book sermons: introductory book sermons, major-theme or central-message book sermons, minor-theme book sermons, biographical book sermons, and key-text book sermons. Any one of these may be applied to the book of Genesis.

A series of sermons of almost any desired length may be developed from Genesis along the line of "firsts." Genesis is a book of firsts: the first universe, planet, life, man, woman, sabbath, covenant, name, marriage, birth, family, sin, and death; the first redemption, language, government, sacrifice, literature, art, music, agriculture, cities—all are firsts to be found in Genesis. One resourceful minister came up with these titles for a series of sermons from Genesis:

The First Manhunt ("Adam, Where art thou?"—3:9)
The First Shutout ("The Lord God sent him forth from the garden."—3:23)

The First Shut-In ("The Lord shut him in."—7:16)
The First Installment Plan ("Jacob served seven years for Rachel."
   —29:20)
The First Insurance Plan ("Joseph insured against lean years in
   Egypt."—41:46–49)

Some of the truly great love stories of the race are in the book of
Genesis. Helpful and appealing series of sermons have been built
upon these: "Bold Eve and Alibiing Adam"; "Faithful Abraham
and Questioning Sarah"; "Timid Isaac and Adventurous Rebekah";
"Gallant Jacob and Lovely Rachel."

Genesis has been the favorite book of the Bible for biographical
preaching. Look at a few of the famous and near-famous names:
Adam, Cain, Abel, Seth, Noah, Methuselah, Enoch, Abraham, Isaac,
Jacob, Leah, Joseph, Judah, and Potiphar. Consider a few titles:

Noah—The Conquest of Cir-
   cumstances
Abraham—The Man Who
   Was God's Friend
Abraham—The Man Who
   Passed Through the Great-
   est Trial

Abraham—The Conquest of
   the Unknown
Jacob—The Man Who Was
   a Convinced Crook
Jacob—The Conquest of Self
Isaac—The Man Who Dug
   Old Wells

If a minister wishes to center on single texts, he has an unfailing
mine in Genesis from which to draw:

God Has Priority ("In the beginning God . . ."—1:1)
The Light of Creation ("And God said, Let there be light: and
   there was light."—1:3)
Earth Is Man's Laboratory ("Subdue it."—1:28)
Good Gold ("The gold of that land is good."—2:12)
God's Concern for the Lonely ("It is not good that the man should
   be alone."—2:18)
Are You Kidding? Did God Really Say That? ("He said unto the
   woman, Yea, hath God said, Ye shall not eat of every tree?"—
   3:1)
The Appeal of Vanity Fair ("Ye shall be as gods, knowing good
   and evil."—3:5)

The Aftermath of Disobedience ("They heard the voice of the
   Lord God walking in the garden."—3:8)
God Calling, Line One ("The Lord God called unto Adam."—
   3:9)
Was Not Spoken of the Soul ("For dust thou art, and unto dust
   shalt thou return."—3:19)
Surprise Cash Audit ("What hast thou done?"—4:10)
Reams of Rainbows ("I do set my bow in the cloud, and it shall
   be for a token of a covenant between me and the earth."—
   9:13)
Money Isn't Everything ("Give us bread: for why should we die
   in thy presence? for the money faileth."—47:15)

In the selection of single texts, the preacher's only difficulty is in
their superabundance.

If the interest is in doctrinal preaching, Genesis is an inviting
book: the doctrine of God, of creation, of man, of sin, of judgment,
of punishment, of worship, of possessions, of human relations.
Genesis is "God's plenty" in the realm of doctrine.

Even these brief suggestions are enough to indicate that a man
may tarry as long in Genesis as he dare. Yet, he may move through
the book swiftly if he so desires. For example, Abraham dominates
a large portion of Genesis. To deal with Abraham in one or more
strong biographical sermons will quickly dispose of a great bulk of
material. Or, the preaching upon some of the great ideas found in
Genesis will make it possible to cover a great amount of material
in a relatively short time. Whatever the preacher's plan, he will have
to preach selectively; he will never be able to preach exhaustively
on the book. It is only a matter, after careful and prayerful study,
of how much time he wishes to spend with this great book.

Each book in the Bible will yield to similar treatment. Certainly,
not all the books are as rich and significant for preaching as is the
book of Genesis. For example, while a man might preach a series
of sermons from the letter to Philemon, still, it can be dealt with
rather fully in one sermon. The book of Psalms will always be an
embarrassment to a preacher because of its wealth; when he has
done his best for the book, the faithful preacher will know that he
has not done the book justice. Still, if he wishes to do so, he can deal

with the book rather effectively by preaching a group of sermons on the different types of psalms. He may select one favorite psalm from each grouping as an example of that type.

In conclusion, look at how a month of preaching through the Bible might shape up on the minister's preaching chart.

JANUARY, YEAR

	Event	A.M.	P.M.	Wed.
1st Week	First Sunday After Christmas Life Commitment Day B Bible Study Week B Covenant Sunday P	Scripture Lessons: Gen. 1:1-25 John 1:1-5 Text: Gen. 1:1 Title: "God Has Priority"	Scripture Lesson: Psalm 1 Text: Gen. 1:31 Title: "Who Do You Think You Are?"	Scripture Lesson: Gen. 3:8-9 Title: "God is Here"
2nd Week	1st Sunday in Epiphany Seminary Sunday P	Scripture Lessons: Gen. 1:26 to 2:1 Rom. 8:22-28 Text: Gen. 1:31 Title: "The Brave New World"	Scripture Lesson: Gen. 1:26-28 Text: Gen. 1:26 Title: "Why Do You Think You Are Here?"	Scripture Lesson: Gen. 3:3 Title: "Sin Is Present"
3rd Week	2nd Sunday in Epiphany Evangelism Supply P	Scripture Lessons: Gen. 2:8-9,15-17 Col. 1:13-20 Text: Gen. 2:16a Title: "Father Knows Best"	Scripture Lesson: Gen. 3:23-24 Text: Gen. 3:23a Title: "Where Do You Think You Are Going?"	Scripture Lesson: Gen. 3:13 Text: Gen. 3:13a Title: "Judgment Is Sure"
4th Week	3rd Sunday in Epiphany Baptist Men's Day B YMCA Sunday P World Wide Service Sunday M	Scripture Lessons: Gen. 3:1-6 Phil. 2:5-9 Text: Gen. 3:6 Title: "The Status Seekers"	Scripture Lesson: Gen. 4:25-26 Text: Gen. 4:26b Title: "What's The Big Idea?"	Scripture Lesson: Gen. 3:15 Text: Gen. 3:15 Title: "Deliverance Is Offered"
5th Week	4th Sunday in Epiphany Youth Sunday P	Scripture Lessons: Gen. 4:1-8 Luke 15:11-13 Text: Gen. 4:1-8 Title: "The Problem Child"	Scripture Lesson: Gen. 4:23-25 (RSV) Text: Gen. 4:23-25 Title: "Do You Think You Own The Earth?"	

7

Preaching to Meet People's Needs

(PLAN III)

The hundred-year-old records of an Ohio church tell of a duly elected church officer designated as "Pointer." It was the responsibility of this person to stand in the pulpit by the side of the minister and "point." As the preacher would throw light upon some particular truth, "Mr. Pointer" would point to some drowsing or indifferent member and cry: "You, there, John Doe, that applies to you! Pay attention!"

Rare is the minister who has not felt the need for such an assistant! But "Mr. Pointer" may have been pointing to the wrong party; his time might have been better spent had he prodded the preacher, rather than the longsuffering parishioner, into awareness. There can be no doubt at one point, however; the sermon should have relevance. The message should speak to the needs of those present. This is an overpowering purpose of the sermon.

And this purpose gives significance to the third preaching plan, "Preaching to Meet People's Needs." A sermon is delivered to deal with real problems of real people. That is a sermon's specialty; it is what makes it a sermon rather than an essay or a lecture. Every sermon should have as its main business the head-on, constructive meeting of some problem which puzzles the mind, burdens the conscience, distracts the life, rejoices the heart, undergirds the faith of the people. "A good sermon is an engineering operation by which a chasm is bridged so that spiritual goods on one side—the 'unsearchable riches of Christ'—are actually transported into lives upon the other." [1]

Not a New Plan

It is not claimed that this view of preaching and what it is supposed to do is new. It is not new. Good preachers have known about it for centuries. Listen to words written by Ralph Waldo Emerson a hundred years ago in his *Journals*.

At church today I felt how unequal is the match of words and things. Cease, O thou unauthorized talker, to prate of consolation, resignation, and spiritual joys in neat and balanced sentences. For I know these men who sit below. Hush quickly, for care and calamity are THINGS to them. There is the shopkeeper whose daughter has gone mad, and he is looking up through his spectacles to see what you have for him. Here is my friend whose scholars are leaving him and he knows not where to turn his hand next. Here is the stage driver who has jaundice and cannot get well. Here is B, who failed last year and is looking up anxiously. Speak, things, or hold thy peace.[2]

Today's preacher, if he is worthy of the name, is a descendant of the Hebrew prophet. And, no one who is even vaguely familiar with that tradition will doubt that Amos, Hosea, Isaiah, Jeremiah, and others of their group, spoke the message of God to real people who had real problems. Now, *there* was preaching according to people's needs! Or, consider the Master himself. It is written that he "came preaching." Yes, and he came preaching to meet the needs of the people before him. He did not preach about the great "First Cause"; he told them that there was a Father God who loved them. He said: "A certain man had two sons." He assured them that not even a sparrow fell without the knowledge of God and that they were more valuable than many sparrows. You will find no metaphysical abstractions or scholastic propositions flung forth to humanity in general. By no stretch of the imagination can you believe that Jesus needed a "Mr. Pointer" to assist him in keeping his hearers awake!

It is also true that at their best the strong preachers in every age have spoken to the needs of their people. Tertullian preached on "The Duty and Benefits of Patience"; Chrysostom preached on

"Excessive Grief at the Death of Friends"; Melancthon on "The Security of God's Children"; Cotton Mather, "The Joyful Sound of Salvation"; Alexander Chalmers, "The Expulsive Power of a New Affection"; Bushnell, "Every Man's Life a Plan of God"; Tallmadge, "The Christian at the Ballot Box"; Henry Ward Beecher, "The Moral Teachings of Suffering"; Thomas Jefferson, "The Sinfulness of Worry"; Charles Reynolds Brown, "Religious Quitters"; George W. Truett, "The Privilege and Peril of Opportunity"; Hugh Black, "Does Righteousness Pay"; Arthur John Gossip, "How to Face Life with Steady Eyes"; Harry Emerson Fosdick, "The Basis of Moral Obligation"; Albert Palmer, "Running Away from Life"; Daniel Poling, "What Men Need Most"; Ralph W. Sockman, "Prejudice"; G. Studdert-Kennedy, "Bread, Work, and Love"; and Robert J. McCracken, "Can Human Nature be Changed?"

Preaching according to people's needs is not new; the Hebrew prophets and Jesus did it, the strong preachers have often done it. A few of these have done it consistently and have followed a purposeful plan in doing it. The fact remains, however, that very little attention has been given to this kind of preaching by the average preacher. There has even been some difficulty in agreeing upon a name for such preaching. It has been called "life-situation" preaching, "problem-solving" preaching, "therapeutic" preaching, and an older name which, when used in a psychological and counseling sense, still takes on much of the significance of such preaching— "pastoral" preaching.

Names are not as important as content. What matters is that shortly after the sermon begins, one listener and then another and another finds "the preacher bowling down his alley." If the sermon content is rich, the entire congregation becomes, as Fosdick says, "tense and quiet, seeing that the sermon concerns a matter of vital importance to every one of them. The preacher was handling a subject they were puzzled about, or a way of living they were dangerously experimenting with, or an experience which had bewildered them, or an ideal they were striving for, or a need they had not known how to meet." [3]

A Needed Plan

When a minister stands before his congregation for the first time after becoming their pastor, he obviously does not know a great deal about the group as individuals. In some ways each congregation is different from every other congregation. The church in the university center is not the same as the church tucked away in a mountain cove, nor is the village church the same as the cathedral church in the heart of the great city. Yet, it is possible to overemphasize differences in churches, for the differences may not be as great as the similarities.

It is safe for the new pastor to assume, as he looks out upon his flock for the first time, that certain characteristics will be present. One of these characteristics will be present to a greater degree in one church, another to a greater degree in another church. Nearly any church will have representatives of the following age groups: babies, children, young people, young adults, the mature, and the senior citizens. There will be those with different abilities. Different economic and cultural levels will be represented. There will be the male and the female; the married and the single; the satisfied and the rebellious; the creative and the frustrated. There will be those whose work is a blessing and others who look upon their work as a curse; there will be those who are happy at home and others who are casting longing eyes toward distant pastures; there will be those who fret because of large families and those who would give all but virtue and self-respect to have children and cannot.

There are Jacobs in the congregation. When Jacob and his brother Esau had been reconciled, Esau suggested that he accompany his brother whom he had not seen for so many years. However, Jacob urged that he not do so, saying: "I will move on slowly, at my leisure, adjusting ourselves [his family] to the pace that suits the endurance of the livestock." The minister may assume that there are those who accommodate themselves to the pace of the livestock rather than to brotherhood. It is true that the dead conscience, the dead heart, the dead soul, as well as the stab of sharp pain and the aching loneliness, have to be included when we affirm that a man reaps what he sows. God does not always punish by sending adversity; he frequently gives the nation or the individual their heart's desire but sends leanness in the soul. This happens in every congregation.

There is courage and beauty in every congregation. Henry Ward Beecher strode to his pulpit in Brooklyn one morning after calling on a dying member on the way to church. The famous preacher's first words were: "It makes me preach like a lion to see how my people can die." The new pastor may assume that some of his people have such ability. J. Middleton Murray wrote in the introduction to the *Journal of Katherine Mansfield,* his wife, the following words: "She suffered greatly . . . She was utterly generous, utterly courageous; when she gave herself to life, to love, to some spirit of truth which she served, she gave royally. She loved life." [4] Mary Carolyn Davies' little poem speaks of a surprise that every pastor has had or will have. She writes,

> Where weary folk toil, black with smoke,
> And hear but whistles scream,
> I went, all fresh from dawn and dew,
> To carry them a dream.
> I went to bitter lanes, and dark,
> Who once had known the sky—
> To carry them a dream—and found
> They had more dreams than I.[5]

As a minister stands before his people for the first time, he is fairly safe in assuming that the above analysis will hold true for the group before him, and for the larger group which is not before him. As he stays with the church, giving himself to his people in the role of a good minister of Jesus Christ, he will be able to document these characteristics. He will be able to give names, addresses, zip codes, and telephone numbers to sins and to virtues. And, he may well say with John Watson, whose pen name was Ian Maclaren, "Be kind, for everyone you meet is fighting a hard battle." And, he may be able to bear the testimony George W. Truett bore as a young man. Young

Truett refused the invitation to become president of a school, saying: "I have sought and found the shepherd's heart."

When a thoughtful minister realizes that his congregation is made up of such diverse characteristics and different needs, he will see how important it is that his plan of preaching take these facts into consideration. He will see that it is not enough to be concerned with objective facts in his sermon. He has to be concerned, too, with the subjective conditions in the lives of his people. It is the preacher's business to so preach the fact of the gospel that the people will hear, heed, and believe, and thereby experience forgiveness, renewal, and power. When these truths were realized by a certain famous preacher, he wrote: "Only the preacher proceeds still upon the idea that folk come to church desperately anxious to discover what happened to the Jebusites."

A Discounted Plan

Increased interest in preaching to meet people's needs is due in no small degree to increasing interest in the field of pastoral psychology although, as stated, the Hebrew prophets were worthy forerunners and Jesus was the perfect example of this type of message.

At the same time, there is much in the latter half of the twentieth century that seeks to discount this type of preaching. At the heart of this discounting is the criticism of the local church. The "quality of life" within the local church and its "ethical and moral poverty of spirit" have been proclaimed by press, radio and television, soapbox, lecture platform, and pulpit. Such words as "irrelevant," "obsolete," "conservative," "reactionary," "clingers to the status quo" are too familiar to need amplification in the context of the church. The following statement is typical: "Organized religion is irrelevant to the major forces which are operative and determinative in American society: it does not affect them, and it relates to them in an overwhelmingly passive way." [6]

As a part of this overall, general criticism of the local church is the specific criticism that centers in and grows out of a social existentialism which maintains that truth is something that you *do*. It claims that the validity of the church succeeds or fails, depending upon its involvement in the social, political, economic, and racial issues of the time.

A more careful reading of the New Testament, of Christian doctrine, of a systematic theology, of church history—to say nothing of a valid experience of the grace of the Lord Jesus Christ within the heart—would correct such a lopsided position. For the church of Christ does not depend upon anything so impermanent and weak as man's ethical and moral excellence. It depends, rather, upon the promises and the power of God made clear in Jesus Christ. It is easy to be led astray by a philosophical concept that is allowed to exercise a controlling influence in the understanding of the place, work, and being of the church. "Existentialism is a helpful idea when used as a tool by Christian faith. However, when it seeks to be itself the standard by which biblical themes are judged, then it exceeds its role of instrument and handmaiden." [7]

This should in no way be interpreted to say that the imperative demands resting upon disciples of Christ in the area of social, political, economic, and racial involvement are unimportant. They are important and they must be obeyed on penalty of disobedience. Punishment for disobedience to God is never to be taken lightly. What is meant to be emphasized here is that God's love for and presence in the churches does not rest upon man's "doing" but upon God's promise and grace. Paul faced this matter in the church at Corinth. As sinful as I am, as sinful as my fellow church members are, I do not believe that the church of which I am a member is guilty of some of the crimes that Paul points out in the church at Corinth. But, let us not forget that Paul still wrote: "You are the body of Christ and individually members of it."

It also needs to be said that when the very validity and being of the local church is called into question because it is not as actively involved in sociological upheaval and change as some feel it should be, a major task and function of that church is being overlooked. Surely, one needs to do his homework more carefully if he is unable to see the private, individual, personal work that the local church is commissioned by her Lord to do. There are areas of personal sin and guilt, of loneliness and meaninglessness, of peace and concord, of sickness and death, and the life everlasting that must be dealt with. A long time ago, Newman said that there was not a man in Europe who was so bold in his criticism of the church but that he owed it to the church that he could speak at all. It might be pointed out, too, that there is scarcely a critic of the church who blasts its lack of involvement in social issues that does not owe it to the church that there are involved volunteers in these movements at all. It is the churches that have, consciously or unconsciously, influenced the leadership. It is the churches that have, consciously or unconsciously, been responsible for opening the financial springs whose waters are so necessary if these deserts are to blossom.

This is no less true in social legislation than in voluntary slum clearance. When the legislative and legal machinery have done their work—work that went back to the churches and the Judeo and Christian teachings and traditions for its motive and influence—the fact remains that "much land remains to be conquered." Without a constant flow of goodwill and respect, this machinery is in for hard sledding. The churches, now and in the future, as in the past, will have to furnish much of this.

So, let the criticism that would discount a planned preaching program based upon people's individual and personal needs (though by no means limited to these), remember that the only way to effectively and ultimately deal with issues, causes, and movements is to deal redemptively with the men and the women who make up these causes and movements. Bishop F. R. Barry once wrote that there was no such thing as Christian action, there were only Christians acting.

A Plan with Dangers

"You cannot escape the temptations of the world or the flesh or the devil even in the cloister; all you can do is to change the form they take." [8] So, to approve, even to be enthusiastic about a preaching plan that seeks to meet people's needs does not discount the fact that there are possible dangers to the use of such a plan. Every preaching plan has its dangers. This approach is not an exception. Consider a few dangers that need to be kept in mind, not to frighten one from using the plan, but to help one to be forewarned with the hope that he may be forearmed.

One may become frustrated over the multitudinous needs of the people and cry out: "Who is sufficient for these things?" The answer is, "No one." No one is adequate to deal with all the problems and needs of a congregation. The number of needs is too great; their complexity too involved; their eradication calls for a skill that the minister does not have.

Surely this would have to be said about any type of preaching. The basic and ultimate source of the sermon—any sermon that is worthy of the name, is God, not the preacher. The preacher is a channel for the message, not its source. The Bible is his test, not the latest book on psychology. This plan of preaching does not dispense with the Bible; it is difficult to think of any kind of preaching that calls for a more constant and skilful use of the Bible.

The plan of preaching according to people's needs may stir up more snakes than the sermon is able to kill. For example, it may be like the popular television program that seeks to help the layman diagnose certain diseases. The local doctor knows that he is going to be flooded with calls from patients who are sure they have the difficulties described by the program, though they were never aware of the difficulty before.

Similarly, when a preacher deals with a particular problem, some individuals may decide that they, too, have that problem, although they had gone on year after year and never recognized it before! However, if the sermon not only diagnoses and describes but goes on to give an honest and positive prescription based upon the Word, will, and purpose of God, the listener may well decide that rather than take the prescription he will not "imagine-up" the symptoms.

A very real danger lies in the area of identification. The minister may so diagnose and describe a problem that an individual in the audience is very sure that his own case is being paraded before the congregation. This is quite different from so dealing with a problem that every person in the audience feels that the sermon has his own name and address on it. A businessman was asked the secret of his pastor's effectiveness in the pulpit. The layman answered: "I never hear him preach but I feel like saying, 'How did he know that I had that need today?'"

Another danger is that the minister may become so timely that his preaching has no timelessness. He may be so eager to speak the language of the layman that he forgets to speak the language of God, so eager to communicate with men of earth that he forgets that his business is to communicate to men of earth the message of heaven. It is easy to become so "practical that one becomes trivial." Watch it! The minister is, ought to be, a minister of the gospel of God, not an amateur psychologist. His business is not to give a lecture but a sermon; there is a difference.

It is also easy to deal with conscious needs and forget about un-conscious needs. This danger is easy to observe. The needs that are felt are the ones that the preacher can most easily identify. But these may not be the most basic needs that the members of his congregation have. Often symptoms will appear while problems remain hidden, hidden to the individual and, unless he is very wise, hidden from the minister. It is often difficult even for the minister with true discernment to say: "Here and here, thou lackest."

Another real danger is that the minister will become more sensitive to the needs of his people than conscious of the resources of his God to meet those needs. One wonders if that is not the difficulty with many ministers today. How else can the discouragement and talk of failure on the part of so many be understood. No matter what problems a man may face, be they his own problems or problems of his people, so long as he has a God who is greater than the problems and the needs, he will not despair. But, regardless of how trivial the needs, if his faith is in a God who is inadequate to deal with the trivial needs, the preacher is still in the throes of discouragement. The minister must not only know his people and their needs, he must know his God and God's resources.

Qualifying for the Plan

How does one get ready to make a year's preaching program based on the people's needs? Obviously, if the minister is to plan his preaching according to the people's needs, he must know what those needs are. How does he get this information? Much of what has been written in this chapter is relevant at this point. While every congregation is different from every other congregation, there is much that is similar in all. In a sense, if a man knows one congregation he knows all. The matter of age, culture, intellect, and talents, the sinner and saint, the lonely, the sad, and the adjusted, may vary in degree and quantity, but the elements are present in every congregation. This is a place to begin. It is not the place to end.

In speaking of the "demon possessed boy," Jesus said that such a case yielded only to prayer and fasting. If the minister is to preach to people's needs, there is information that he can get only through being a *faithful pastor*. This kind of planning and preaching can only be done effectively by the man who lives with his people, lives with them in length and in depth. That is, a long pastorate is required, and during the long pastorate the pastor must become deeply involved with his people.

Here, as in other areas, the ministry of Jesus is the shining example. For, while he was not a pastor in the sense that is meant here, his involvement with people has not been surpassed.

He shared with them their common lot. He became a part of the life of his generation. He seemed to belong to them. He dragged the sorrows of his generation across his soul. He could not keep himself out of the welter and misery of men. Their problems were his problems, their dilemmas were his dilemma, their pain was his anguish, their disappointment was his sorrow. At midnight it was a Hebrew scholar; at daybreak it was a foundering ship; at noontime it was a fallen girl at the well; in the afternoon it was a hungry crowd of the unemployed. Across the threshold of his home in Capernaum there fell the shadow of the limping and the lame, the halt and the blind. And he healed them all. He identified himself with the paralytic who had just enough feeling to know pain. He became one with the lepers whose bodies withered with anguish. He seemed to belong to the blind who stumbled through the streets of eternal darkness. He cared what happened to the lily that faded, the reed that was bent, the coin that was lost, the prodigal son who had stepped across the threshold of indiscretion. He was the most compassionate man who ever lived.[9]

And so, the good pastor has his people in his heart and keeps them there; he claims identity with them in joy and sorrow, in all the vicissitudes of life. The good gift bestowed upon one makes the pastor stronger; the suffering found in any household makes him the poorer; if a young man stands against strong temptation, the pastor is strengthened; if the young man falls, the pastor is the weaker; if a young woman shows distinguishing marks of grace, the pastor thanks God as for himself; the pastor watches eagerly for the prodigal to turn his face homeward; the pastor rejoices with the father when the fatted calf is killed; the pastor watches over the youth who has special gifts. The pastor is slow to criticize for he understands, and to understand is to forgive; and the love he has for his people covers a multitude of their sins.

The minister who would preach to people's needs must needs be a pastor. Let him have something of the heart, spirit, and service of Goldsmith's village parson and he will have many of the qualifications for preaching to his people's needs. In "The Deserted Village" Goldsmith wrote,

> Thus to relieve the wretches was his pride,
> And ev'n his failings leaned to virtue's side;
> But in his duty prompt, at every call,
> He watched and wept, he prayed and felt, for all;
> And, as a bird each fond endearment tries
> To tempt its new-fledged offspring to the skies,
> He tried each art, reproved each dull delay,
> And lured to brighter worlds, and led the way.

When John Frederick Oberlin was pastoring his flock for the Lord in the Vosges Mountains of France, he let it be known that he would be in prayer one full hour of each day for his people. During that hour he would be praying for them by name. As the people passed their pastor's house during that hour, heads were bowed, voices were silent, spirits were reverent. Their faithful pastor was lifting them on the strong wings of prayer up, up to God.

When the greathearted Dick Sheppard of St. Martins-in-the-Field,

London, died, his people knew that it was for them that he had lost his life. He sat up all night with his people in their illness. He loaded himself with the burdens of others; he succored those who had never known a tenth of the suffering of the man who was bearing their sorrows. He spent himself on people; he literally lost his life for them. Naturally, he had great influence with the people. When he died they found themselves talking, not about their great love for him, but about his great love for them. One of the East London dock workers cried out: "Good Gawd, Mother, what shall we do without 'im?" Dick Sheppard could, and did, preach to people's needs.

The Importance of Study

There is another requirement for the minister who would preach according to his people's needs: it is that he be a man of books. He must be a student. He may not be a great and brilliant scholar, but he can be a lifelong student. He needs to be a lifelong student of the Bible. The Book yields her treasure only to those who love her and who give to her their undivided attention. He must be a student, too, of doctrine. In the context of his people's needs the doctrines of sin, grace, forgiveness, love, atonement, redemption, and salvation will not be hoary with age and dust, but instead will breathe the breath of life into glad and tragic human situations.

The minister who preaches according to his people's needs must be a student of human nature. He faces two dangers in the study of books on psychology and counseling. One is that he will not give adequate attention to them; the other danger is that he will lose himself in them and believe that such studies can meet all his people's needs. Folly lies in the direction of each procedure. But, used rightly, this field of study has help to offer that the minister can get nowhere else.

The minister who would do this kind of preaching needs to read and study biography. The field of great biographies is an indispensable one for such preaching. Here one sees more than ideas, ideals, principles, and precepts. Here is life—life with worthy ideas, ideals, and principles put into practice. As the minister enters vicariously into the lives and the work of the great, he takes on greatness.

The carefully planned, skilfully worked, and diligently executed survey can furnish valuable information for preaching according to people's needs. The people do not always know what their greatest needs are, but if a minister is wise and kind he will endeavor to learn what his people believe are their real needs. Indeed, if he does not do so he may thereby indicate a deep need in his own life!

From living the life of a good pastor, from living the life of a conscientious student, from living with his God and with his people and with his books, and through careful surveys, the minister can plan a worthy preaching program to meet his people's needs. While the list below may indicate the negative, each subject in the list should be dealt with positively, constructively, curatively.

Life	Insecurity	Anger
Death	Inferiority	Resentment
Ill health	Pride	Doubt
Emotional disorders	Prejudice	Tension
Guilt	Loneliness	Injurious habits
Sorrow	Meaninglessness	Covetousness
Alcohol	Defeat	Competition
Grief	Immaturity	Family problems
Handicaps	Communication	The aged
Eternal life		

In Thornton Wilder's thoughtful play *Skin of Our Teeth*, Mrs. Anthropos pleads with her husband to get back the promise of bringing something good out of that which is bad. She says that that hope and that promise were all that kept them going in the past and that he must get it back. It is not comfort they want; they can bear any suffering that is necessary. But they must believe that something good can come out of it all. Mr. Anthropos answers: "All I ask is the chance to build new worlds and God has always given us that. And has given us voices to guide us, and the memory of our mistakes to warn us . . . We've come a long ways. We've learned. We're learning. And the steps of our journey are marked for us." [10]

Let this chapter close with something of the same faith. Something good, lovely, and beautiful can come out of trouble. God gives the promise; he gives the Holy Spirit to speak and to guide. "We've learned. We're learning. The steps of our journey are marked." Let us go forth to preach to the people's needs.

FEBRUARY, YEAR

	Event	A.M.	P.M.	Wed.
1st Week				Need: Dedicated Leadership Title: "Leaders Must Lead" Scripture: Mal. 1:6 to 2:9
2nd Week	5th Sunday in Epiphany Race Relations Sunday Boy Scout Sunday P YWA Focus Week B	Need: Preaching to the Purposeless Title: "Born for Such an Hour" Scripture Lessons: Esther 5:13-16 Eph. 1:1-12 Text: Eph. 1:4	Need: Preaching to Those Who Feel Inferior Title: "Never Sell Yourself Short" Scripture Lesson: Matt. 16:21-27 Text: Matt. 16:24	Need: Lay Evangelists Title: "Power Charged Circuits" Scripture: Acts 1:1-8
3rd Week	6th Sunday after Epiphany Day of Prayer for Students P Seminaries, Colleges, and Schools Day B	Need: Preaching to the Prejudiced Title: "How Goes the Race" Scripture Lessons: Psalm 139:1-12 Eph. 2:13-22 Text: Eph. 2:13-14	Need: Preaching to Those Who Need Forgiveness Title: "Forgive—Or Else" Scripture Lessons: Matt. 18:23-35 Text: Matt. 18:35	Need: Lay Evangelists Title: "Learn By Doing" Scripture: Mark 1:14-20
4th Week	1st Sunday in Lent Boy Scout Sunday P World Service Sunday M	Need: Preaching to the Lonely Title: "The Loner Is Lonely" Scripture Lessons: 1 Kings 19:4-18 Acts 9:36-41 Text: Eph. 3:1	Need: Preaching to the Selfish Title: "When the Lid Blew Off the Id" Scripture Lesson: Acts 8:14-24 Text: Acts 8:19	Need: Lay Evangelists Title: "Tell It Loud and Clear" Scripture: James 1:19-26
5th Week	2nd Sunday in Lent	Need: Preaching to Those in Pain Title: "Suffering That Saves" Scripture Lessons: Isa. 53:1-12 2 Cor. 12:1-10 Text: Isa. 53:3-5	Need: Preaching to Those Who Feel Guilty Title: "Give Your Guilt a Goal" Scripture Lesson: Isa. 1:11-18 Text: Isa. 1:18	

8

Preaching by Months

(PLAN IV)

"Time," wrote Thomas Mann in *The Magic Mountain*, "has no divisions to mark its passage, there is never a thunderstorm or blare of trumpets to announce the beginning of a new month or year. Even when a new century begins, it is only we mortals who ring bells and fire off pistols." Right on both counts! Time has no divisions, but mortals do. Man does mark time.

The fourth preaching plan takes this into account. It is planning your preaching according to months. The plan is marked by what it does not do as well as by what it does. It does not follow a central theme or emphasis throughout the year as do the plans already mentioned. When the plan of preaching is by months, the emphasis is upon twelve units of time for the year's preaching program. There may be a carry-over in preaching and in Scripture lessons from month to month, but this is not basic to the plan. The plan calls for working in and through twelve units of time. Actually, there are twelve monthly preaching programs that fit together to make the one year's preaching program.

It must be kept in mind, of course, that whatever plan is followed, much of the material used will be the same. Whatever the plan, certain days, seasons, and emphases will need to be taken into consideration—Christmas, Easter, Thanksgiving, missions, stewardship, and evangelism, for example. The particular plan that is followed in the preaching program will determine the how, the when, and the relatedness of the material. One plan will give more freedom, while another plan will insure a more disciplined and structured approach.

Advantages of the Plan

Planning your preaching by months has certain obvious advantages. It is probably the easiest plan to project and to follow. It is much easier to plan a program that takes into account four or five weeks than it is to plan a program that provides for fifty-two weeks.

In the second place, much of our thinking and living is compressed into monthly units. Many salaried people are paid on a monthly basis; they pay bills on a monthly basis; they borrow on a monthly basis. Schedules in the home, office, and school often center about the month. Church plans are made according to months, and social hours, banquets, and promotion use the monthly theme and motif.

Again, by working with the month as a unit of time, the preacher has more freedom of control, structure, and emphasis. Novelists claim that once the sails are set, the goals chosen, the seamen (narrative characters) taken aboard, the writer is no longer free. He has to let his ship of fiction sail according to plot and character development. Something of the same can be said for preaching the Christian Year and preaching straight through the Bible. Choice there is; a preacher is not a slave to the plan. Yet, to the degree that he follows the plan he will be held within bounds. The same is not true, certainly not to the same extent, when a minister is preaching according to months.

Notice, too, that this plan offers greater variety in choice of materials and emphasis. In a letter written to Annie Webster on the first day of September, 1876, Mark Twain commented on the weather in New England as follows: "There is a sumptuous variety about the New England weather that compels the stranger's admiration—and regret. The weather," he continued, "is always doing something there; always attending strictly to business; always getting up new designs and trying them on people to see how they will go." The humorist said that in the spring in New England he had counted one hundred and thirty-six different kinds of weather within the space of twenty-four hours. While that might be just a little too much variety for preaching, regardless of plan, still, if the minister desired it, preaching according to months might qualify him for that league.

Another advantage of such a plan lies in the use that it can make of all other plans. When one is preaching according to months, he is free to roam at will and select any good thing that he desires from all other programs. Charles Lamb once remarked that the human species was divided into two groups, men who borrow and men who lend. The preaching that makes use of months as planning units may well borrow more than it lends. And, finally, it is easy to preserve the results of all homiletic gleanings when one uses this plan. Probably with no other preaching plan can the minister so easily file materials and be sure of their ready accessibility as when he is preaching by months. The reason for this will be seen when the details of the plan are set forth later in this chapter.

Disadvantages of the Plan

Not everything about preaching according to months is on the asset side. There are possible disadvantages. One, there is no guarantee that the minister who follows the plan will preach the full gospel of Christ. And whatever else a minister is required to do in his preaching, and he is required to do many things, he certainly is required to preach the whole gospel.

True, no plan absolutely guarantees this desired result. But one is more likely to achieve it if he follows carefully the Christian Year, or if he preaches straight through the Bible. However, preaching the whole gospel can be done according to months, and it can be done better according to months than according to weeks, which is what most ministers do.

Second, there is the danger that the preacher may rob his people of the blessings of a carefully planned program for the public reading of the Scriptures. Again, this is not to say that it is impossible to have a worthy plan of Scripture readings; but if a man's preaching plan is made on a month to month basis, he is less likely to have a worthy and continuous program of Scripture readings than if his preaching plan were continuous for the full year.

Akin to the above dangers is a third. In preaching according to months, (i.e., by blocks of time rather than by majoring on themes), a minister may minimize the periods of preparation leading up to the major events in the life of Christ and in his gospel. It was noted in an earlier chapter that more time is often spent in preparation for the great events in the Christian Year than is spent on the events themselves when they appear. The Advent season and Christmas are examples. While a person would certainly emphasize Christmas and Easter through the monthly plan, it would be easy for him to slight the important preparatory periods which help us to appreciate the deep significance of the events themselves. This preparatory emphasis is very important if a minister wishes to have a strong teaching element in his preaching. Teaching requires time; often it is built line upon line, precept upon precept; here a little, there a little. It cannot be done with a quick hit and a near miss.

And, finally, let this fourth danger be pointed out: it is easier for a minister who preaches according to months to become a chaser of fads, to be a mere seeker after the novel and current, even secular emphasis of the day. This need not be so—certainly not—but it is a danger that is ever before the minister who uses the plan. Preaching needs to be interesting; there is no virtue—there may be sin—in dulness. However, a preacher should never have as his goal to be merely interesting; the sermon is not primarily for the purpose of entertainment.

Lady Mary Wortley Montagu was a delightful letter writer and charming society figure of the eighteenth century. Her last words were these: "It has all been very interesting." The final evaluation of life and our role in it should be more than that. Certainly a man's preaching should be more. Let the preacher beware; no chasing after fads and mere novelties, please.

Techniques of the Plan

Calendars play a large part in preaching according to months. Constance, in Shakespeare's *King John,* wanted to know what a certain day had done that it should be set in letters of gold "among the high tides of the calendar." One of the first tasks in preparing this preaching plan is to put down the days in the calendars that are set in gold. The days should be selected from several different calendars, including the Christian calendar, the denominational calendar (denomination-, state-, and association-wide), the civic, and the local church calendar.

As a careful study is made of these, something like the following list of days may be selected for the first three months of the year. (Some of the events are variable and will not fall on the same day, or even in the same month.)

January

New Year's Day, January 1
Epiphany Eve, January 5
Epiphany, January 6
January Bible Study, 1st full week in month (SBC)
Week of Prayer, 1st full week in January (Protestant)
Soul-winning Commitment Day, January 9 (SBC)
Church Anniversary Service, January 16 (Local)
Baptist Men's Day, January 16 (SBC)
Youth Week, January 30–February 5 (Protestant)

February

Baptist World Alliance Sunday, February 6 (SBC)
Race Relations Sunday, February 13
St. Valentine's Day, February 14
YWA Focus Week, February 13–19 (SBC)
Brotherhood Day, February 20
Universal Day of Prayer for Students, February 21 (Protestant)
Baptist Seminaries, Schools, February 20 (SBC)
World Day of Prayer, February 25 (Protestant)
First Day of Lent, February 27 (Protestant)

March

Week of Prayer for Home Missions, March 6–13 (SBC)
Home Missions Day in Sunday School, March 13 (SBC)
Youth Week, March 13–20 (SBC)
Passion Sunday, two Sundays before Easter
Palm Sunday, one Sunday before Easter
Holy Week, beginning with Palm Sunday
Maundy Thursday, Thursday of Holy Week
Good Friday, Friday of Holy Week
Easter Sunday
Life Commitment Sunday, March 20 (SBC)
Evangelistic Services, March 27–April 3 (Local)

A careful checking of the calendars for the year should reveal something similar to the above list of days and events for the remaining nine months of the year. The making of this list should be the first step in planning a preaching program according to months. This does not mean that all the days and seasons that are set in "letters of gold" will be used as bases for sermons. Some of these will be entirely ignored, some will be referred to in passing, some will be used for illustrative purposes. But they need to be noted in the preaching plan.

Then, with fifty-two folders, one for each Sunday of the year, each can be marked for a particular month and Sunday, such as January, 1st Sunday; January, 2nd Sunday, and so on. Into each folder should be placed three work sheets (discussed in an earlier chapter) —one for the morning service, one for the evening service and one for the midweek service. Later, if it appears that the material for three services is becoming too bulky for one folder, additional folders—one for each service—may be added.

With the material selected from the different calendars before him, the minister can now choose days, seasons, and emphases that he wishes to make use of in his preaching program. These he can place on the appropriate work sheet in the particular folder, whether the emphasis is to be made on Sunday morning, Sunday evening, or at the midweek service.

Now, with twelve larger folders, one for each month, marked January through December, the weekly folders can be placed with the appropriate month. This is the beginning of the twelve monthly working units for the preaching program. From this point on the work will be largely by and within these individual units. If the work has been done carefully up to this point, a surprisingly large portion of the year's preaching program has already been designated.

If the program thus far seems mechanical, the minister may remind himself that at some time during the year, in one way or another, he would want to deal with most of these items. It comes down to a matter of long-range planning as to the *when* and the *how* of the emphasis. In fact, this is probably the only way that the minister will deal with many of these items, even though he knows that the education and nurture of his people merit the instruction. It is only through planning ahead, through reading widely and gleaning materials ahead of time that the preacher will feel adequate to deal with the events when they arise.

At this point a careful and honest survey should be made of the past year's preaching program. With honesty as his guide, the minister will have to admit that there were gaps in his preaching program during the past year. He will also be forced to admit that his own special interests, reading habits, and local circumstances caused him to give undue emphasis to certain areas of his preaching. He will find, too, that he has subjects, titles, references, and illustrations in his previous year's files that were never used.

A careful survey of the past year's preaching program will give him much grist for the coming year's program. Now is the time to transfer this material from the past year's files to the coming year's program, to the appropriate files and work sheets. This will mean, in some cases, further filling in of unchosen dates in the program. In some cases it will be a matter of feeding the files that have already been marked from the calendars.

Of one thing the preacher may be sure: no good idea, concept, illustration, or written paragraph will ever be wasted. Do the work; write it down; tuck it away. It will be needed and it will be used.

Series for the Plan

After the calendars and last year's preaching program comes series and courses and individual sermons. The minister will find that by this time the Sundays are beginning to come with a "price upon their heads." Series will need to be shortened or broken, for there will not be sufficient space for a long series.

This may be a good thing; it is easy to make the series too long. This is truer for the preacher than for the audience. The audience tires of a series that is too long; however, it is largely the tiredness of the preacher that tires the audience. It is difficult for the preacher to maintain his interest in and excitement over a series that goes beyond a few sermons. And it is all but impossible for him to hide his state of mind from his audience. Emerson said that nothing great was ever accomplished without enthusiasm. Let the series be short and well placed.

As in other preaching plans, the series may be for the Sunday morning service, the Sunday evening service, or for the midweek service. There will probably be more freedom in the Sunday evening service. The major emphases from the calendars will usually be dealt with in the morning services, although some of these events may be better for the evening service. Say, for example, the emphasis is on a civic or national concern, such as Brotherhood Sunday. The minister would like to reach the power structure in his city— the mayor, the city councilmen, the judges, the lawyers, the school administrators—regardless of their church affiliation. The chances for reaching them will be better in the evening service than in the morning service. Many of these individuals will be, it is hoped, in their own churches for the morning hour of worship. By the same token, they will be free from their own churches in the evening. Their churches may well be dark on Sunday evenings, or lighted only for youth groups. Because of this, these people will more readily accept a special invitation to attend other churches in the evening. Too, it is the kinder thing to do. Ministers of the other churches will react more favorably to their people participating in other services if those services are at a different time from their own.

A series of sermons on Sunday evenings in February might be based upon Christian patriotism and other national interests. February is known as the month of great men. It is the month when the birthdays of Lincoln and Washington are observed. A series with the general theme, "The Message of the Church," would be appropriate: "The Message of the Church on War," "The Message of the Church on Race," "The Message of the Church on Brotherhood," "The Message of the Church on Patriotism." Such a series, if wisely planned, effectively promoted, firmly grounded in the Scriptures, and carefully anchored to history and Christian tradition would reach a large segment of the community and influence it for good.

The "Preach It Again" series has been effectively and helpfully

used for the Sunday evenings in January. I made this a regular
feature of my preaching program for many years. In November
or early December, the titles of the sermons preached during the
year were printed and submitted to the congregation with the request that each person indicate the five sermons he would most
like to hear repeated on the Sunday evenings in January. The results of the voting were then tabulated and the five sermons receiving the largest number of votes were preached on the indicated
evenings.

This is an excellent way for the minister to check up on his own
preaching. And it is a fair assumption that he will be surprised at
what is revealed. For example, every sermon title listed will receive
at least one vote; some of the sermons that the preacher felt were
the least helpful will receive a larger number of votes, while, con-
versely, some of the sermons he felt were his best will receive
low ratings. If on some Sunday the preacher was pressed for time,
some unexpected, unavoidable interruption cut his preaching time
to ten or twelve minutes, he will find that a disturbingly large
number of people will feel that it was his best sermon! Sermons
that took some unusual approach, contained dramatic incident, or
had some strong life situation worked into them will rate high in the
favor of the people.

If the preacher will study carefully such a survey once each year,
he will learn much about his people and his own preaching. Such
a study may mean more to him than a refresher course in the
seminary; it may well change his preaching patterns and change
them for the good.

June is a good month for strong series of sermons on romance,
marriage, and home. June has long been known as "the month of
weddings." The Bible is only a few pages old when it comes to
grips with this important matter. Some of the best-known love
stories in the world are those of the Old Testament. If a man needs
further assurance as to the appropriateness and importance of the
emphasis, let him consider that when God showed his love toward
us in its most dramatic form, it was through the door and relationship of a home.

Some years ago it was my privilege to preach for a week at a summer assembly at Ridgecrest, in the Blue Ridge Mountains of North Carolina. Night after night the audience numbered an average of thirty-five hundred people, fifteen hundred of whom were Intermediates, ages thirteen through sixteen. The remainder of the group was composed of varying ages. A large element was made up of the lay and professional leadership from the churches. Night after night the sermons were based upon the great love stories of the Bible. The messages were little more than a careful retelling of the stories, with an endeavor to put them in something of a present-day form. The reception on the part of the entire group, but especially the thirteen- to sixteen-year group, was convincing proof that such series are relevant and greatly appreciated.

July and August are difficult months for preaching. In many areas of the country the weather is uncomfortable. Many of the people are away on vacation, others are planning to leave, many are wishing that they could get away and are unhappy because they cannot. They long for the mountains, the sea, the great "wide-open spaces." In planning his preaching program according to months, the preacher would do well to plan a series of sermons that catch something of the spirit of God's great out-of-doors. This has often been done with helpful results. A series of sermons extending over a month based on "God's Men and Their Mountains," would stimulate the minds and imagination of the people. It is not often realized how many of the great events recorded in the Bible took place on mountains: Noah and Mount Ararat, Abraham and Mount Moriah, Moses and Mount Sinai, Gideon and Mount Gilead, Saul and Mount Gilboa, Elijah and Mount Carmel, Christ and Mount Calvary, the ascending Lord and the Mount of Olives.

Another stimulating month's series of sermons for the summer may be based on "God's Knights of Night." Consider, again, how many of God's great acts took place at night, how many of his knights performed great deeds during the hours of darkness. Let a few chosen sentences of Scripture indicate the rich ore that waits to be mined by the thoughtful and resourceful preacher:

"He [Jacob] dreamed, and behold a ladder set up on the earth, and the top of it reached to heaven: and behold the angels of God ascending and descending on it" (Gen. 28:12).

"So Gideon, and the hundred men that were with him, came unto the outside of the camp in the beginning of the middle watch (Judg. 7:19).

"About midnight the shipmen deemed that they drew near to some country" (Acts 27:27).

"There were in the same country shepherds abiding in the field, keeping watch over their flock by night" (Luke 2:8).

"Peter went out, and wept bitterly" (Luke 22:62).

"It was night" (John 13:30).

"Being in an agony" (Luke 22:44).

"There shall be no night there" (Rev. 22:5).

Years ago Charles E. Jefferson, pastor of the Broadway Tabernacle, New York, preached and later published a series of helpful sermons using the same general theme of nature. He entitled the series "Nature Sermons." The individual titles were "The Rainbow," "Deserts," "Birds," "Sunsets," "Storms," "Shadows," "Sounds," "Mists,' "Spring," "Odours," "The Landscape," and "Lakes."

In *Alice in Wonderland* Lewis Carroll tells of the lock that went running around with the cry, "I'm looking for someone to unlock me." That may be said of the Bible. Great biblical preaching is waiting for the man who carefully plans his preaching by months.

Earlier in this chapter it was pointed out that the minister who uses the plan of preaching according to months runs the danger of chasing after fads and embracing that which is merely new, the danger of forsaking the great body of the gospel and Scriptures.

Herb Caen, well-known columnist for the *San Francisco Chronicle,* is fiercely loyal to his city, San Francisco. Recently he let loose the following blast:

The critics are falling on the city fang and claw these days. "San Francisco lives in the past," is the endless refrain (so what else is old?)—and all I can say is that it's nice to have had such a past to live in. The texture of a city is drawn from its beginnings, and the tapestry that is San Francisco is strong in legends; turn your back on them, laugh at them, and the fabric begins to tear, the colors blur, and the hard-won accolades—"The city that was never a town"—turns to dust.[1]

Lift that magnificent word to the height of the holy Scriptures and take it from there!

Reading and Storing for the Plan

By the time a minister reaches this spot in planning his preaching program, he may be ready to cry, "My kingdom for a free Sunday!" For, if he has done his work with all the calendars and with the previous year's preaching program, if he has carefully planned and filled in his series of sermons, he probably has few if any gaps left. The gaps that remain can be filled in with ideas for sermons, texts, subjects, and suggestions that he has gleaned from his reading, his pastoral work, and his living. These he will have noted in a book or on carefully preserved cards.

He now has a file for each week in the year; into each of these files have gone three work sheets: one for Sunday morning, one for Sunday evening, and one for Wednesday evening. On these work sheets have been listed dates, subjects, and, in some cases, titles, Scripture verses, and ideas. These weekly files containing the work sheets have been placed in the appropriate monthly file, so that he now has all of his material in twelve folders, each marked for a particular month. What next?

He is now ready to begin feeding these files. If the minister will spend one hour each week in reviewing his work sheets, he will find that much of what he reads, hears, sees, and experiences will immediately relate to his preaching program. Suggestions and materials can be noted on the appropriate work sheets; clippings from daily papers or written paragraphs can be dropped in the right folder; his reading and study of the Scriptures can be noted on the work sheets; and suggestions for a sermon outline can be made. As the program gets under way, a good idea or illustration that he was unable to use in one sermon can be carried forward to the appropriate file for a future sermon.

By the time the minister begins his preaching program in January, assuming that he started his planning the summer before, he will find that when he comes to a particular Sunday and the designated emphasis for that day and service, he already has much of his work done. He will have done much of his reading and research, biblical and otherwise. The structure of his sermon has already taken form; ideas for getting the sermon under way, illustrations to serve as windows upon truths and principles, are waiting for his use. Chapters in books, articles in magazines, sources for biblical word studies, choice exposition in favorite commentaries are listed on his work sheet, title and page number awaiting his quick reference.

With this much of his work done, with so much material awaiting his use, the minister can give himself to careful, concentrated thought—something many ministers are not able to do when they come to prepare a weekly sermon with no previous effort having been given to it. When Solomon was ready to build the Temple in Jerusalem, he uttered some words that the preacher can apply to the preparation of his sermon when he has carefully done his "homework" beforehand. Solomon said: "The house which I built is great, for great is our God above all gods."

What a motto for a minister to have on his desk as he begins to write his sermon! Great preaching is possible when the planning is done according to months.

MARCH, YEAR

	Event	A.M.	P.M.	Wed.
1st Week		———	———	**Series: Great Chapters** "The Gift of God Chapter" John 3
2nd Week	3rd Sunday in Lent Girl Scout Sunday P Week of Prayer for Home Missions B	——— Title: "A Nation Whose God is the Lord" Scripture Lessons: Joel 2:12-17 Matt. 6:16-21	——— Title: "How Does The Cross Save Us?" Scripture: Luke 23:33-43	"The Love of God Chapter" 1 Cor. 13
3rd Week	4th Sunday in Lent Youth Week B	——— Title: "Accent on Youth" Scripture Lessons: Josh. 24:14-24 Eph. 6:10-20 Text: Josh. 24:15	——— Title: "Our Eternal Contemporary" Scripture: Heb. 13:1-8 Text: Heb. 13:8	"The Shepherd of God Chapter" Psalm 23
4th Week	5th Sunday in Lent Church Anniversary (Local) One Great Hour of Sharing	Title: "Our Past Proclaims Our Future" Scripture Lessons: Isa. 28:14-16 Acts 13:44-49 Text: Rev. 3:8	——— Title: "On Lifting Up A Standard" Scripture: Isa. 62:1-10	"The Comfort of God Chapter" John 14
5th Week	6th Sunday in Lent Passion Sunday Associational Youth Youth Night B	——— Title: "Palm Branches And Cross Beams" Scripture Lessons: Zech. 9:9-12 Phil. 2:5-11	——— Title: "On Swinging Your Lantern Higher" Scripture: John 1:35-42	"The City of God Chapter" Rev. 21

9
Denominational Emphases
(PLAN V)

Most denominations have a schedule which they have agreed upon—sometimes called "The Denominational Calendar." This program is proposed by a group of representative pastors, laymen, and denominational administrators. These men determine which theme or themes, events, special seasons, or emphases it would be wise for the churches to promote, and these events are arranged in the most desirable order for the year ahead. This program of work or calendar of activities is then presented to the proper executive groups, assemblies, or convention for approval, modification, or rejection. When the program is adopted, it becomes the program of the entire denomination.

Through whatever media are at its command, the program is then promoted. An effort is put forth to secure the approval and active participation of all pastors and churches. The following explanation gives the spirit and intent of one such program:

The Denominational Calendar is designed to suggest to the churches significant emphases and events which may be observed during the year. It also indicates the times when related materials will appear in the denominational publications. These suggestions are made with the understanding that each church, association, and denominational organization will choose emphases and events in keeping with its own needs.[1]

A student participating in a march of protest on a university campus recently was seen carrying the following sign: "I am a student; do not fold, bend, or mutilate." It is not difficult to see that a denominational program is adopted in the full knowledge that pastors, churches, and institutions are jealous of their right to decide *what, how, if,* and *when* such a program will be followed.

The above statement clearly says: "The Denominational Calendar is designed to *suggest.*" In most Protestant denominations, the calendar is a suggestion, not a law; pastors and churches may use their discretion. The program sets forth "significant emphases and events which *may* be observed during the year." Again, there is no obligation. If, one the other hand, the suggested calendar is followed, there will be assistance in the form of helpful promotion and useful materials for implementing the program.

Finally, in order to avoid any possible misunderstanding, the statement concludes: "These suggestions are made with the understanding that *each church, association, and denominational organization will choose emphases and events in keeping with its own needs.*"

A Commendable Idea

Such a program has much to commend it as the basis for a plan of preaching. Consider: It is proposed by a reliable and representative committee. The committee is composed of pastors, church laymen, and responsible denominational representatives. It is logical to assume that these individuals have the welfare of persons, churches, organizations, institutions, and the denomination as a whole uppermost in their minds. In addition, they have at their disposal information in the form of special opportunities that it would be difficult for an individual minister to have in his possession —opportunities which the committee has spent much time weighing and evaluating. They have sought to see single needs in the context of all needs and to look at the whole in the light of individual claims. It is on this basis that the program was first proposed. This first proposal was followed by a careful scrutiny by different individuals, groups, and the denomination-at-large in conference.

In the second place, the program specifically recognizes that the calendar will need to be used according to church, organizational, and institutional needs; the needs are not all the same. The program will not be used in the same way by all concerned. The right of individual choice is recognized and affirmed.

Again, the program makes clear that there are distinct advantages in cooperation. There are certain needs, emphases, and seasons that all ministers feel it is wise to observe sometime during the year. It is difficult for anyone to see how the gospel can be preached, the needs of God's people and the sins of men addressed, without giving careful attention to these.

Then, if a minister's preaching program has to include these sometime during the year, why not make the emphases in cooperation with others? There will be occasions when this is not wise, but as a working rule, with wise foresight and careful planning, such situations can be cut to a minimum. As noted above, there will be supporting materials in the denominational publications at this time; often, articles and features will appear in secular publications or on radio and television.

Often, there is value in having a large segment of the entire Christian community thinking, conversing, reading, and praying about concerns of mutual interest at the same time. If some unpopular ethical and moral issue needs to be faced, it can be faced with less friction and more effectiveness if all ministers in the community face it at the same time. "In unity there is strength." Dr. Temple once wrote: "But when we come to what we can do ourselves, it always seems so little, as, of course, it is. What each one alone can do is always very little, but the way great things are done is by all doing that very little together." [2]

Notice further the educational value of coordination. Emphasis is being made simultaneously in all areas of the educational program of the church. The church is stronger for presenting a united approach in its teaching and proclamation. If both the Sunday School and the pulpit, for example, emphasize missions, evangelism, or stewardship, the coordination is advantageous to both.

One reason our churches are not more effective is that there is not enough concentrated effort. Preparation of the soil, planting of the seed, cultivation of the crop, careful harvesting and marketing are all necessary to good farming. A football player once assured his coach, the famous "Hurry Up" Yost of the University of Michigan, that the team was sure to win on Saturday because the players had "the will to win." "Hurry Up" answered: "Don't fool yourself. The will to win is not worth a plugged nickel unless you have the will to prepare." That is equally true in preaching, and the preparation calls for more than the preparation of the sermon—it calls for a preparation of the people.

The preacher needs to remind himself, also, that the carefully prepared denominational program provides a well-balanced diet for the nurture of his people. The program may be lacking in some areas, but in the main the emphasis is inclusive. A program that I have before me now emphasizes missions, evangelism, education, stewardship, vocational choice, Christian literature, social ministries, prayer, Bible study, music, men, women, youth, children, race relations, health, denominational heritage, and the local church.

And, notice, the above is from the denomination's national calendar only. The minister who plans his preaching program according to his denominational program will add his own state denominational program, his associational denominational program, plus his local church program. These four calendars need to be studied carefully and need to be carefully coordinated in building a preaching program.

Some of these programs show an annual theme, also valuable in planning the preaching program. The following are examples:

1965–1966: "A Church Fulfilling Its Mission Through Proclamation and Witness"
1966–1967: "A Church Fulfilling Its Mission Through Education"
1968–1969: "A Church Fulfilling Its Mission Through Ministry"
1970–1971: "A Church Fulfilling Its Mission Through Evangelism and World Missions"

In addition to the annual theme, there is a special emphasis for each month that gives broad but valuable suggestions for a preaching program. And, in some cases, these programs are projected five years in advance. While a few changes in the program need to be made from year to year, the program will give the minister opportunity for all the effective long-range planning that he can desire in his preaching.

A final advantage in planning a preaching program according to the denominational program is this: it contributes to a healthy and creative approach to the people's own denomination. Whatever a preacher's personal inclinations may be toward his own and other denominations, their separation or their togetherness, there is need for the people to be informed about their own denomination. It is not through lack of appreciation for one's own denomination that a worthy appreciation of other denominations is developed; the reverse is true. It is only through an intelligent love for one's own communion that he can appreciate the love that his neighbor has for his communion. It is the person who is secure in the knowledge of his own tradition and its contribution who has patience and courage to hear of the traditions and contributions that other groups have made.

It is tragic to see a pastor and people acting as if they are ashamed of the denomination of which they are a part, only a cowardly spirit keeping them from breaking all connections with it. Where such is the case, it may safely be assumed that part of the blame lies at the door of the minister in not properly informing his people of their own denomination, its history, contribution, and program. Woodrow Wilson spoke to that truth when he said, "A nation which does not remember what it was yesterday, does not know what it is today, nor what it is trying to do. We are trying to do a futile thing if we do not know where we came from or what we have been about." That is no less true of a denomination than it is of a nation.

Obvious Dangers

No plan of preaching is without dangers; this one has pitfalls in abundance. One danger should be obvious: it lies in the substitution of means for ends.

The purpose of any plan is to aid the minister to more effectively preach the whole gospel of the "blessed God." The preaching of the gospel is the end; the use of the denominational program or calendar is the means. After considerable experience with those who are responsible for the formulation and projection of the denominational programs, I am confident that this is the purpose that motivates their efforts.

This, however, is no guarantee that the program will be so used. The program may be used for its own sake. Its total acceptance and its complete promotion for its own sake may become the yardstick by which a man gauges his own success or failure in the ministry— *i.e.*, not the spirit and the content of his preaching but the carefulness with which he follows the denominational calendar in his emphasis.

Another danger attendant in the use of this preaching program is that it may become the standard by which a minister gauges not only his own effectiveness but also the effectiveness and worth of other ministers. If a fellow pastor follows closely such a plan, he is a loyal and a reliable leader; if he does not follow such a preaching plan, he is neither loyal nor reliable.

In the early days of our country most places of business had what was known as a "counting room." It was a place in the store, factory, or business where the books were kept, the accounts balanced, evaluations made, where future procedures were agreed upon. In a preacher's "counting room," when evaluations are made of his brethren, too much importance may be attached to whether these brethren push the right buttons and sound the right notes, and all in unison.

This is, of course, an error that the power structure of a denomination, as well as the individual minister, may fall into. It is fearfully easy for those who are charged with the responsibility of promoting a denominational program to look with undue favor upon those who also are especially diligent in promoting that program.

Early in January of 1966 the Vatican published a decree listing conditions by which Roman Catholics might receive plenary (full, entire, complete, absolute) indulgence during the church's special jubilee that ran from New Year's Day to May 29. It is interesting to note that, according to the Associated Press, each of the con-

ditions listed by Pope Paul VI had to do with some act closely connected with the church's life and machinery. The five were as
follows: attending a three-part series of instruction connected with
the ecumenical council held in Rome by the church; listening to
sermons on the council during a three-day mission; attending a
solemn mass said by a bishop in a cathedral; visiting a cathedral
during the jubilee, or another church named by the bishop, and
making a profession of faith while there; and, finally, receiving a
papal blessing conferred by the local bishop during a solemn
ceremony.

Two notations may be made: (1) The granting of indulgences
did not stop when Martin Luther did his nailing job at the cathedral
door; (2) the Roman Catholic Church gives special attention to
those who promote her own ecclesiastical welfare.

There is little danger that Protestants will be guilty of the error
of proclaiming that pardon can come to an individual through something that he does on his own. Surely the Bible undergirds Martin
Luther at that point. But, in giving approval to those who adhere
strictly to adopted programs—and for little reason beyond that—we
may not be above blame.

Another danger that faces the man who uses this program for
preaching is that the form may become so tight in structure that
there will be little opportunity for the Holy Spirit's full guidance
or for a man's own ideas, initiative, and originality. True, this same
danger is present in the use of any form, but it may be more
present in the use of the denominational form. Forms do not necessarily oppose a man's own ability nor the work of the Holy Spirit.
Ideally, forms should be an aid to both, but the ideal is not always
realized.

Sometimes music is written with certain "blanks" in the com-
position. The blanks are there intentionally, indicating a sort of
"do-it-yourself" spot. In the performance of the whole it is up to the
flutist, the trumpeter, or the violinist to make his own contribution
at that point in the performance. Every preaching program must
make room for such initiative.

On Tuesday evening, November 23, 1965, there was consterna-
tion in the town of Lulea, Sweden. Actors on movie screens began
to perform in reverse, oil that was being taken from tanks in the
harbors began to flow back into the tankers, pumps at service
stations began taking gasoline out of tanks of cars and forcing it
back into the pumps. Machinery in general began to run in reverse.
Explanation? An engineer had thrown a wrong switch on the line
leading from the hydroelectric dams high in the mountains! Watch
it, preacher! Do not let that happen as you plan your preaching
according to the denominational plan.

To sum up the advantages and the dangers, then, of using the
denominational program as a basis for one's preaching program, let
this be said: There are dangers that a minister needs to guard
against. However, these dangers are not in the plan itself; they are
in the misuse of the plan. The advantages of the plan far outweigh
the perils that misuse of the plan may bring. Most of the dangers
are possible with the misuse of any plan. A careful, prayerful use of
the plan can bring great benefit to the minister and his people, and
effectiveness to a man's total preaching ministry.

Available Techniques

The techniques for setting up this preaching plan are similar to
those designed for other preaching programs. With the four denominational calendars before him—national, state, associational,
and local church—the minister begins his work. He places themes,
emphases, seasons, and days of the denominational calendars side
by side. He chooses those he thinks merit attention in his preaching
program for the coming year and eliminates the others. The parts
of the calendars that remain are combined and coordinated for
effectiveness. (Much of this has already been done in working out
the calendars. The responsible representatives on the national,
state, and associational levels have worked closely in formulating
the calendars.)

When this has been done, the material is placed on the annual
civil calendar. A large portion of the fifty-two Sundays will thereby

be claimed. However, there will be gaps, open dates. Besides, some of these themes and emphases can be dealt with in one of the weekly services, some can better be handled in another. The Sunday morning hour of worship will claim the major portion of the material, but the Wednesday evening hour will claim some and Sunday evening, others. In some cases, each of the three services will need to emphasize the same theme. There will be certain national days that should receive attention in any preaching program; some of these—for example, Lincoln's and Washington's birthdays, Fourth of July, Labor Day, Veterans Day—will be accented one year and some another year.

With the annual preaching calendar before him, now marked with all the special days, seasons, and emphases that he has chosen, the preacher can fill in the free blocks with individual sermons that have been germinating and sprouting in his mind and notebook. These "seedlings" had their origin in the preacher's devotional study of his Bible, his general reading, his pastoral visitation and counseling, and his awareness of the political, social, economic, business, and entertainment fields.

Every annual preaching program should have several courses and series of sermons. These will be placed on the preaching calendar in relationship to the denominational calendar. He may preach a series of sermons on evangelistic themes in January, since January may be the time when the theme "Everyone Win One" is current, or when "Soul Commitment Day" is observed.

Another series or course of sermons, may be preached in February on Christian patriotism, brotherhood, or God's Word on present-day issues. Another year a special series may be preached on education: education in our homes, our churches, our public schools, colleges, universities, and seminaries. This would be in keeping with the emphasis on the denominational calendar for February. March and December would be an excellent time for special sermons on missions, since March is the month the denominational calendar gives special emphasis to Home Missions and December is the month when attention is given to overseas missions.

Whatever time is available in April could most certainly be used for an extended preaching emphasis upon life commitment and vocational choice. This is an area that receives great attention in the Scriptures and is of crucial concern to all who are interested in the future of the churches and of Christian missions, as well as to all institutions that have their existence beneath the banner of Christ. The denominational program calls attention to this truth.

For years attention has been focused upon the inadequate enrolment in our seminaries and divinity schools. This is the case not just for one denomination but for all—Jews, Catholics, and Protestants alike. Many surveys have been made; diagnoses have been published. There can be little question but that one of the basic causes goes back to the local church. The challenge, the adventure, the service, the rewards are not held before the youth of the churches by the ministers. Frankly, there is not enough outright claim placed upon the lives of the young by the pastors.

There is ample idealism on the part of the young. Indeed, as one looks at the way the youth of the land are giving themselves to all kinds of causes—from the Peace Corps and antipoverty program to all kinds of crusades—it may be wondered if the great problem does not lie in the failure of ministers to appeal to the idealism of youth. While many causes are stepping up their appeal to idealism, the churches are easing up on theirs.

In Shakespeare's *Henry IV* Falstaff cries: "God, God, God." The attendant says: "I bid him that he should not think of God. I hoped that there was no need to trouble himself with such thoughts yet." The time has come, the night is far spent, when the youth should be reminded, repeatedly and insistently, to think of God's call upon their lives. Let the preacher follow his denomination's calendar and preach the great truth.

May and June would be an excellent time for a series of messages on friendship, marriage, and the home. May is the month for Christian home emphasis, and, of course, June is the month of weddings. October and November should have special emphasis in the field of stewardship and budgets.

Limited Time

By this time the preacher will be ready to cry, "My kingdom for free days and hours to preach relevant and vital themes." The themes that he has used, as well as those he can find no place for, are mainly in keeping with the denominational calendar. Through various forms of literature and promotion, his denomination has made its contribution; and, in this way, the people have been conditioned and prepared for the preaching program.

The preacher will get assistance from another source when he uses the denominational program as a guide to his preaching program: denominational personnel. This includes secretaries of the different phases of the work, missionaries (home, state, and overseas), presidents, and representatives from the different institutions. A church may get "too much of a good thing" in the use of outside representatives. But the minister should assist his people to become acquainted, firsthand, with these servants of God and of the denomination.

It is easy for people to feel very impersonal about their giving to and support of the causes that their denomination sponsors. One of the best ways to personalize missions is to put names and faces to the programs.

My wife and I have tried to take advantage of every opportunity to meet our missionaries. We have had them in our home and church on numerous occasions. One day we were talking to our children about vocations and how important it was that they let God guide them in the selection of their life's work. A direct question was put to our six-year-old by one of the other children: "What are you going to be when you grow up?" She answered: "I am going to be a return missionary."

Of course, our six-year-old did not understand what she had said. (No doubt many would like to have the "return," provided they could get it without going out and serving.) What she did see was that her home and church considered it a privilege to host those who had been to the mission fronts of the world. She got the idea that they were important people and naturally enough, she wanted to be like them.

Help will come from another source in the use of this program. It will come from effective promotional channels that are open to the preacher. It has already been emphasized that periodicals and other types of denominational literature would feature the themes of the denominational calendar. No thought has been given, however, as to how effective this fact can be in securing an audience for the preached word.

Many individuals have a mistaken, if not false, modesty about this part of their ministry. If a sermon is helpful to a hundred people, surely it would be helpful to five hundred. And if a man helps only a hundred people when he could help five hundred, he needs to seek forgiveness from God! If a sermon does not reach and influence an individual, the sermon might as well not have been preached so far as that individual is concerned. Surely a man should use all good and reputable means at his disposal to enable people to hear the gospel. Let the preacher apologize if he does not do this.

It is not easy to persuade people to give heed to the gospel. People are busy, they are satisfied, they are comfortable, they are indifferent to the realm of the spiritual. The problem has been set forth recently by a popular columnist in one of the country's great newspapers. He wrote this:

Beautiful, blond and luscious Joan Hitchcock had reason for feeling euphoric a few mornings ago. It was her 33rd birthday, and her husband, Fremont Brodine (Peter) Hitchcock, had just presented her with a diamond as big as the Fairmont. Her children were all well and happy. Things were going splendidly at the ranch they own in Santa Rosa, and they were off in a few hours to their house in Palm Springs.

Humming a merry tune, she put on her mink-lined sable, or perhaps her sable-lined mink, and walked out of the Hitchcocks' $250,000 mansion on Broadway, stepped into her chauffeur-driven limousine, and went to the St. Francis Medallion Room, where Mrs. Arthur Dettner was honoring her at a birthday luncheon. When the birthday cake arrived, candles aflame, Mrs. Dettner said, "Make a wish, Joan."

A long silence followed. The candles burned lower and lower.

At last Joan looked around at the circle of expectant faces and said helplessly, "Honest—I can't think of a thing." [3]

The columnist, I presume, did not mean to cast any unkind reflection on the lovely lady who was having the birthday; certainly no unkind personal reflection is meant here.

On the whole, ministers will not be dealing with many individuals who fall in that economic bracket. But, make no mistake, the same spirit of comfort and satisfaction and complacency possesses those with whom the ministers deal. It is not easy to make them aware of their hunger and need for God. If the preacher can do it he owes it to them, to himself, and most of all to God in Christ to do it. The task will call for skill. The sons of this world have been wiser in their generation at this point than have the sons of light.

Some years ago a woman in Knott County, Kentucky, was leafing through an unused Bible. In it she found a $100 World War I Liberty Bond dated 1918. The accumulated interest made it worth $146. The tragedy was not that the Liberty Bond had been lost, but rather that the Bible had been closed so that wealth far surpassing $146 had been locked in from circulation.

It is the contention of this chapter that one of the avenues to opening the Bible so that its treasures may circulate among the people is through the effective planning of a preaching program according to the denominational calendar.

APRIL, YEAR

	Event	A.M.	P.M.	Wed.
1st Week	Palm Sunday Life Commitment and Church-related Vocations Month B	Title: "God Believes In You" Scripture Lessons: Ezek. 37:1-10 1 John 5:4-10 Text: John 1:42	Title: "Abraham: God's Call to Faith" Scripture Lessons: Gen. 12:1-5 Heb. 11:8-10	Title: "The Satisfaction of the Christian Life" Scripture: Phil. 1:3-26
2nd Week	Easter Sunday Jewish Fellowship Week B	Title: "For Heaven's Sake" Scripture Lessons: Ezek. 34:11-16 1 Peter 2:20-25 Text: 1 Cor. 6:20	Title: "Moses: God's Call to Freedom" Scripture Lessons: Ex. 3:7-10 John 8:31-36	Title: "The Ideal of the Christian Life" Scripture: Phil. 1:27 to 2:30
3rd Week	1st Sunday after Easter Cooperative Program Day B	Title: "A Declaration of Dependence" Scripture Lessons: Isa. 49:14-18 2 Cor. 1:3-7 Text: Matt. 6:11-13	Title: "Daniel: God's Call to Worship" Scripture Lesson: Dan. 6:1-23	Title: "The Energy of the Christian Life" Scripture: Phil. 3 to 4:1
4th Week	2nd Sunday after Easter National Christian College Day P & M	Title: "You Bet Your Life" Scripture Lessons: Isa. 63:7-9 James 1:17-21 Text: Matt. 16:26	Title: "Paul: God's Call to Preach" Scripture Lesson: Acts 9:10-16	Title: "The Newness of the Christian Life" Scripture: Phil. 4:2-20
5th Week				

10
Evangelistic Preaching
(PLAN VI)

From one point of view, all Christian preaching is evangelistic preaching. For, unless preaching is biblically based, unless it proclaims the Word of God, unless it asks for a response on the part of the hearer, it is difficult to see how it can be called "Christian preaching." The Christian sermon may deal with the kerygmatic facts of the gospel story, it may treat some relevant moral issue of the day, it may proclaim some great promise inherent in the gospel. Regardless, the sermon, if it is a Christian sermon, moves toward a verdict, a decision, a response on the part of the listeners, and that response stems from a confrontation with God in Christ. When that confrontation does take place, there has to be a response. The response may be positive, it may be negative—but response there must be. As the old gospel song had it, "Neutral you cannot be." In that sense, all Christian preaching is evangelistic preaching.

It may be said (and, I think, not without truthfulness) that this note and this spirit should pervade all preaching, and that when it does, you have evangelistic preaching. It may be said that an evangelistic sermon is not so much a certain type of sermon as it is a certain spirit of a sermon. Evangelistic sermons do not rely upon a certain organization in their structure, not even upon certain types of texts, but upon purpose, motive, and intent.

Defining the Terms

There is, however, a sharper, more restricted sense in which we speak of evangelism and evangelistic preaching. In this sense, to

118

evangelize means to center your attention and message on the "outsider," on the individual who is not a member of the household of faith, who is not a committed part of the believing community. "To evangelize," in this sense, "is to so present Christ Jesus in the power of the Holy Spirit that men shall come to put their trust in God through Him, to accept Him as their Saviour, and serve Him as their King in the fellowship of His Church." [1]

It seems that a careful reading of the New Testament would convince any honest man that this was the main business of the early Christians. To be a Christian meant that one was committed to winning the pagan world around him. The early Christians were not playing the part of witnesses; they *were* witnesses; they *were* ambassadors; they *were* representatives. To cease to so perform was to cease as Christians. When they sought to evangelize, they were just doing what was natural to their new nature. In the oft-quoted military words "Conquest has made me and conquest must sustain me," the early Christian would have changed only one word, "conquest," to "evangelism."

Only in this context can we understand the spirit, action, and achievement of the young Christian movement. Harry Golden has said that if a religious survey had been taken in the Roman Empire in A.D. 65, it would have shown the following results: for Jupiter, 51 percent; for Zeus, 30 percent; for Mithra, about 9 percent; for Jesus, about 1 percent. Golden said that St. Paul could have looked at those statistics and said, "The heck with it"—then gone home. But Paul and the others stayed, stayed as evangelists; and that made the difference! When we preach as evangelists, we are getting back to grass roots.

Specifying the Need

There are special considerations that give impetus to evangelistic preaching today. And, strange as it may seem, the impetus springs from those very conditions that are usually given as argument against evangelistic preaching. *First*, it is said that the *whole* approach of evangelism is foreign to today's thought and spirit. (As for this being a culture that is not sympathetic to Christian evangelism, there has never been a culture that was friendly to Christian evangelism. Certainly the culture of the Roman world during the first three centuries after Jesus was not!)

Yet, there has never been so much of the "evangelistic" method employed as is being used today. It is not Christian evangelism, but it is a strong, aggressive, outreach to the last man. This is true in the realm of political philosophies, of business enterprise, of educational outreach, of sports and entertainment, and of health and poverty programs.

Second, it is said that the world does not know, it does not understand, it does not care what the churches are talking about when the evangelistic message is proclaimed. There is, of course, some truth in this, and there always has been. Yet, the church has managed to make its message understood to its own day and generation. It can do so again.

There is another word to be said, however. The basic problem of opposition to the evangelistic note is not that the secular world does not understand; the opposition comes from the very fact that the world *does understand,* and all too well. It knows, just as the world knew in the first centuries, that the evangelistic message, when it is faithfully proclaimed, is against everything that the culture of the day holds to be of greatest value. The preaching of the cross today, as in the first century, is a stumbling block and just plain foolishness to the current culture.

But since when was this a justifiable reason for ceasing to be evangelistic?

There is a *third* consideration that makes the evangelistic note so necessary in worthy preaching today: the strong tendency in certain areas to remove God and Christ, law and gospel from the center of all ethical and moral thinking. In the place of these great, value-determining realities, man becomes the sole value. Man is placed at the center. Whatever ministers to man is good; whatever does not minister to man is not good. What is good for man cannot be determined in advance of the particular situation in which we find man; what is good for man cannot be determined by any outside value. It is the right here, right now, with this particular man in this particular spot that determines action.

The proclaimers of the "situation ethic" can make their case sound plausible enough. They can even call on the great New Testament word "agapé" for support. Does not "agapé love" mean just this, that you love an individual solely on the basis of what he needs to have done for him? You do not love him on the basis of what he can do for you or on the basis of some exterior command.

In First Place

There are two notes in all great evangelistic preaching that speak to this position. First, agapé love never claims that its action is based on what the beloved *wants* or *desires;* it does not base its actions on *sympathy* for the beloved. Rather, this love is based on what the loved one needs. What the individual needs is based on who the individual is, and who he is is determined by his relationship to God. Thus, the individual's needs have to be determined on a theological basis, not on a sociological, cultural, or political basis.

A second note important here is that God and not man is at the center of life. Evangelism denies that our first consideration is man, it says that our first consideration is God. It denies that we should love our neighbor *in the place of* God, or that we should love him *as* we love God. It says instead that we are to love God with heart, soul, mind, and strength, and then to love our neighbor not as we love God but as we love self.

The clear implication is that we shall not know how to love self acceptably until we love God first. God is first—all other loves are based upon, derived from, born out of that. The words of Roger Hazelton are to the point: "It is one thing to meet the world on its own ground, it is a different thing to meet the world on its own terms." The first is appropriate, the second we must never do. We meet the world of the neighbor on God's terms.

Evangelistic preaching has not been free of all faults, but it has consistently placed God at the center of all value-determining judgments. Great evangelistic preaching has declared that man could not save himself; man could not save his brother, no matter how much he loved the brother, no matter how completely he became involved with the brother. Salvation is God's business and he sets the terms; he has not abdicated that authority.

Consider a *fourth* great need that worthy evangelistic preaching speaks to. This need is closely akin to, yet different from, the one just discussed. This consideration grows out of the confusion that is being caused by the social existentialists. It is contended that the very existence of the churches depends upon their becoming involved, committed in the social, political, cultural movements of society—that herein, and herein alone, the church proves its relevance, shows that it is in truth the church.

According to this view, no proclamation of the "mighty acts of God," no true piety toward the Lord Jesus Christ, no praying for the "consolation of Israel," no preaching peace to the captives or deliverance to the guilt-laden, no faithfulness to the "bride of Christ," no proclamation of the fulfilment of God's purpose in Jesus for individuals who accept him through saving faith. None of this has any relevance. All that matters is that the church become "involved in the social situation." This, and this alone, will save the church from extinction.

I suppose we have gotten beyond the days when the cry of heresy might be heard in the land. Otherwise, surely this would be a good time to raise it. Since when does the existence of the church depend upon man's works rather than upon God's faithfulness and his promises? He promised to be where his people were; he promised a secure existence to his church. Where is the chapter and the verse that says that presence and existence depend upon man's works?

Here we come upon a strange bit of reasoning. The social existentialists are quick to declare that wherever the people are, the church must go. The church must not turn from the people; it must become identified with the people. The greater the sin (they might not use that word) the more important it is that the church be there.

But, see what happens? The creature becomes more virtuous

than the Creator. God, they say, will definitely forsake the church if the church does not "do the truth" (and they have some very definite rules for interpreting what "doing the truth" is). But the creature must not forsake his brother no matter how low, depraved, vile, pathetic he may become.

The words of the apocryphal writer speak with fine irony here: "I said, 'Speak, my lord.' And he said to me, 'Are you so very much distracted over Israel, or do you love him [these people] more than his [their] Maker does?'" (2 Esdras 5:33)

The genuine insight of the critics of the parish church that social obedience and relevance is crucial to its life turns into a misplaced concretion when it is applied to the existence of that church. This misplacing comes about because a philosophical concept is allowed to exercise a controlling influence on the development of a doctrine of the church. Existentialism, particularly in its revised form of social existentialism, is a helpful idea when used as a tool by Christian faith. However, when it seeks to be itself the standard by which biblical themes are judged, then it exceeds its role of instrument and handmaiden.[2]

There is a *fifth* great need for faithful evangelistic preaching. It is seen in the alarming disregard for individual responsibility. We have come upon a day when the stewardship of personal life has reached what seems to be an all-time low. No matter what crimes are committed, the "experts" are on hand to explain it, to analyze it, to rationalize it, to place the blame on society and remove it from the individual who performed the act. There has been little if any effort to apprehend and condemn the senseless and utter disregard for decency, law, and order that went on in the looting of Watts, a suburb of Los Angeles, in 1965. Every attempt has been made to place the blame upon a system, a police force, a society, a governor's office. Every attempt has been made to excuse the murder of individuals in Mississippi, in New York, in Chicago.

Of course, iniquity is a vast pool into which we pour our sins and guilt, just as righteousness and justice are a great reservoir from which we draw our protection. No one would deny that there are many elements involved in such tragedies, and sincere efforts must be made to correct the system. The fact remains, however, that *individuals* hurled rocks through the windows in Watts and put the torch to buildings and overturned cars; *individuals* pulled the triggers of the guns, wielded the clubs, and threw into Negro churches the bombs that killed little children. Individuals did these things, and these individuals are guilty. If we are ready to excuse crime because of provocation, any crime can be excused.

What does this have to do with evangelistic preaching? In social existentialism the individual was ignored; here the individual needs to be faced with responsibility. There the individual had rights; here he has responsibilities. True evangelistic preaching will accent again, "Adam, where art thou?" "What hast thou done?" No alibi was accepted in the Garden. Neither would Christ allow Peter to hide behind another. He asked, "[What] if I will that he tarry till I come, what is that to thee? follow thou me." "The soul that sinneth, it shall die," was a word that the prophet spoke for God. It needs to be spoken again, and faithful evangelistic preaching speaks it.

Will Durant, the philosopher, said: "In my youth I stressed freedom and in my old age I stress order. I have made the great discovery that liberty is a product of order." Mark Van Doren says it in his poem "Let There Be Law":

> Wherever earth is home for men,
> Beyond what mountains, by what seas,
> Let honor and pride live; but now
> Let there be law, transcending these.
>
> Let there be law throughout all the world,
> Whose children love their ancient lands;
> May that love grow, but in the shade
> Of justice's most mighty hands.
>
> Let those be guardians of our strength,
> Lest in long anarchy it cease.
> May something deathless now be born.
> Let law be father of our peace.[3]

Respect for the Church

There is a *sixth* great need in the current situation that worthy evangelistic preaching in the local church would go far toward remedying. Again, it is a part of the overall problem that the past few pages have dealt with—the current fad of "religionless Christianity." This is "religion" outside the church—the disregard for, even contempt for, the church in all of its traditional expressions.

Paul condemned the Corinthians for "despising" the church of God. He certainly was not referring to the present form of "despising" the church; it may well be that the present form is far more dangerous. Paul did condemn the Corinthians for bringing shame and disgrace upon the church of God, and it must be admitted that he had abundant cause. Still, let it not be forgotten that in spite of all the despising by the Corinthians, Paul still called the church "the body of Christ." That is something the modern "purists" are far from doing.

Of course, the local church, the "parish church," is imperfect; it will continue to be imperfect as long as there are imperfect men in it. Were it perfect, it would refuse to admit sinful men, including caustic critics; were they received, it would cease to be perfect with their reception or the reception of any other sinful man. But, it may be asked, when did God require perfect instruments for his service? Luther was quite sure that God could carve from rotten wood and ride a crippled horse; he still can; he still does. The carving and the riding does not depend upon the wood and the horse so much as it depends upon God. A functioning, imperfect church is better than a nonexistent, perfect church.

There is a *seventh* need for evangelistic preaching in the local church: the pastor has to preach the whole gospel to his people. He is not free to serve up half a Christ because of the tenderness of certain souls. This full gospel needs to be proclaimed in every church.

The pastor may question the wisdom of evangelistic preaching, for he may not have the lost, the unchurched, in his congregation. To that, two replies may be made. First, the full gospel needs to be preached. There is something in the heart and life of every individual that needs to hear the whole gospel proclaimed. The Christian needs to hear the good news of God's grace proclaimed no less than the non-Christian needs it. The Christian needs to be reminded again and again of the grace of God that lifted him from the miry pit and set his feet upon the solid rock. It may well be that he will hear and see in such preaching an area of his own life that he has never allowed that grace to possess. He may learn that actually he has never yielded his life to God. It would be a wonderful thing if there could be evangelistic revivals *within* the churches as well as *without* the churches.

There is a second word that needs to be said when it is contended that there is no need for evangelistic preaching because the unattached no longer come to our services. It may well be that that is just why they are not in the services. So often our preaching is narrowly gauged to the ear and the concerns and interests of Christians, and only to a restricted number of these. I once had a friend who held that if there were no foxes on a plantation or ranch, all you needed to do to get them there was to get a good pack of walker foxhounds. He said a fox likes to be chased. If the unchurched found a relevant word in our services, they might be willing to come to hear it.

So often our preaching is general. Some years ago I read a book which described one of its characters in this way: "Though she was born honest, she has become adept at squealing, 'You must come to dinner soon.'" There is quite a difference between discussing the advantages of a dinner party with everyone and saying to an individual, "Won't you be my guest for dinner next Thursday evening at seven?"

There is an *eighth* reason for evangelistic preaching and that is numbers. Bishop Charles Gore once said that love was the ability to read statistics with compassion. That is a great observation. One of the reasons many churches and pastors have been frightened away from evangelism lies in the taunts that are hurled at them about numbers—numbers and statistics.

Of course, the pastor should be interested in numbers; if he is not, he should apologize to the Lord God who called him to be a shepherd of sheep. The Good Shepherd was certainly interested in numbers—not just the first, but also the last. He was not satisfied with his flock so long as there was one that was not of it.

Statistics represent persons, and persons are children for whom Christ died. Let the pastor learn to read statistics with compassion and he will not be so easily frightened by the jibes that he is "only interested in statistics." Besides, every frightening statistic about the exploding world population urges us to be passionate evangelists. For every day at setting sun there is a smaller percentage of the world's population marching under the banner of the Lord Christ than was marching under it at sunrise of that same day.

It has been said that English author Jane Austen was so enamored of eighteenth-century English domestic life that she neglected to look out the window and see the French Revolution. It is time that the churches heard the words of their Lord: "He that hath ears to hear, let him hear." The world was once won to Christ through evangelism; if the churches lose the world it may well be for want of evangelism. Can we doubt that every promise claimed by the Christians of the first three centuries when they were winning the Roman world for Christ is ours today for the claiming? Yet, one wonders if even God does not grow weary of offering his saving grace and keeping power when man refuses to accept it. Surely he is God and not man or he would say: "Claim it, or forget it! Claim your right and power and authority as my evangelists or I shall withdraw my promised resources."

John H. Jowett once said: "Many a man who says of some cause, 'I began to lose interest in it, and so I gave it up,' ought rather to say, 'I gave it up, and then lost interest in it.'" This may well apply to many who look with disdain or indifference upon evangelism. New methods and approaches are certainly in order. But if a minister gives up the hot heart and the loud trumpet in the realm of evangelism, there is reason for him to recheck his credentials as a preacher of the gospel.

Surely the preacher must believe that man needs God, that all men need God, that all men need God at all times and in every circumstance. The preacher must believe that God is revealed to man through Jesus Christ. How can any minister preach the gospel of God if he does not believe that the saving grace of God revealed in and made available through Jesus becomes man's own possession through faith, commitment, and obedience? If the preacher believes these great facts, how can he fail to be an evangelist?

The Moral Condition

There is a *final reason* why worthy evangelistic preaching is seriously needed and is so very relevant for the present day. It is the reason that is usually stated first in a call for evangelistic preaching. This need resides in the tragic conditions of private and public morals. The Gold Medal Award of the Freedom Foundation for editorial writing was won in 1965 by the *San Francisco Examiner*. It sets forth the present moral plight as few pieces of writing have. Let its word speak of the need for worthy evangelistic preaching:

The Appalling Erosions of Moral Standards

What has happened to our national morals?
—An educator speaks out in favor of free love.
—A man of God condones sexual excursions by unmarried adults.
—Movies sell sex as a commercial commodity.
—Book stores and cigar stands peddle pornography.
—A high court labels yesterday's smut as today's literature.
—Record shops feature albums displaying nudes and near nudes.
—Night clubs stage shows that would have shocked a smoker audience a generation ago.
—TV shows and TV commercials pour out a flood of sick, sadistic and suggestive sex situations.
—A campaign is launched to bring acceptance to homosexuality.
—Radio broadcasts present discussions for and against promiscuity.
—Magazines and newspapers publish pictures and articles that flagrantly violate the bounds of good taste.
—Four-letter words once heard only in barroom brawls now appear in publications of general distribution.
—Birth control counsel is urged for high school girls.
Look around you. These things are happening in your America.

In the two decades since the end of World War II we have seen our national standards of morality lowered again and again.

We have seen a steady erosion of past principles of decency and good taste.

And—we have harvested a whirlwind. As our standards have lowered, our crime levels and social problems have increased.

Today, we have a higher percentage of our youth in jail . . . in reformatories . . . on probation and in trouble than ever before.

Study the statistics on illegitimate births . . . on broken marriages . . . on juvenile crimes . . . on school dropouts . . . on sex deviation . . . on dope addiction . . . on high school marriages . . . on crimes of passion.

The figures are higher than ever. And going higher.

Parents, police authorities, educators and thoughtful citizens in all walks of life are deeply disturbed.

They should be. For they are responsible. We of the older generation are responsible.

Our youngsters are no better and no worse than we were at the same age. Generally, they are wiser. But—they have more temptations than we had. They have more cars. They have more money. They have more opportunities for getting into trouble.

We opened doors for them that were denied to us. We encouraged permissiveness. We indulged them. We granted maximum freedoms. And we asked for a minimum in respect . . . and in responsibility.

Rules and regulations that prevailed for generations as sane and sensible guides for personal conduct were reduced or removed. Or ignored.

Prayer was banned from the schoolroom and the traditional school books that taught moral precepts, as well as reading, were replaced with inane banalities of "Dick and Jane."

Basically, there are just two main streams of religious thought in these United States. Those who believe in a Supreme Being. And those who do not.

The first group far outnumbers the second. But—this nation that was founded on the democratic concept of "majority rule" now denies the positive rights of many to protect the negative rights of a few.

As prayer went out of the classroom so, too, did patriotism.

No longer are our children encouraged to take pride in our nation's great and glorious past.

Heroes are downgraded. The role played by the United States in raising the hearts and hopes of all enslaved peoples for a century and a half is minimized.

We believe this is wrong. We are convinced that a majority of our citizens would welcome an increase in patriotism and prayer and a decrease in the peddling of sex, sensationalism, materialism and sordidness.

In a few days the *Examiner* will present the first in a series of profiles of our nation's heroes. We will salute the men and women who contributed so much to our national legacy in valor, science, education, religion and art.

In the months ahead we will also intensify our efforts to fight back against the appalling vulgarization of sex.

We do not propose prudery. Neither do we propose wild-eyed, fanatical patriotism.

In both areas, we propose to address ourselves to the problems as we see them with calm reason and respect for the rights of those with views contrary to ours.

As a newspaper we have an obligation to reflect life as it is, not as it ideally might be. We will, therefore, continue to print all the news. That which is sordid and tawdry we will treat in a manner suitable for a family publication.

Over the years we have refused to accept advertising which we felt exceeded the bounds of good taste. We will pursue this course with greater dedication in the future.

Our test will be our own standards of good taste. We do not claim infallibility. Readers have felt we erred in the past. Others will undoubtedly feel we do so in the future. Such errors of excess—if they occur—will be in spite of our efforts. Not because of them.

If the general public is as deeply disturbed as we are by the decline in national morals and in national pride, let it speak out.

Together we can put down the sex peddlers without lifting the bluenoses. And, with God's help, we can put prayer and patriotism back in our classrooms. And in our hearts and homes, as well.[4]

Identifying the Content

This, then, indicates what the content of the evangelistic sermon needs to be. The content of the evangelistic sermon can be stated in different ways. First, there is a great act on the part of God, the gift of his Son. Second, there is a great need on the part of man because of his sin. Third, there is a great offer on the part of Christ, salvation. And last, there is a great opportunity on the part of the Christian—daily life lived in fellowship with God and in service to man.

The kerygma, the sermons of Peter and Paul recorded in Acts and spoken of earlier in this book, are evangelistic in content. Analyze that preaching and you come up with a message that bears the following points: The prophecies have been fulfilled and the new age has dawned in the coming of Christ. Christ, born of the seed of David, went about doing good. He died according to the Scriptures, and the purpose of his death was to deliver us out of this present evil age. He was buried and rose on the third day, even as the Scriptures said he would. He has been exalted to the right hand of the throne of God, exalted there as the Son of God, Lord of the quick and the dead. He will come again both as judge and Saviour of men. Therefore, said Peter and Paul, repent. This was the message that turned the world upside down, or rather, right side up.

In Peter Abrahams' book *Tell Freedom*, a brilliant, sensitive, and discerning young Negro tells of the hardships and persecution he experienced in South Africa. He reveals how he learned to write. He said that when he used clumsy and meaningless sentences, his teacher would say to him: "Read the Bible if you want to see how good English sentences should be written." He said: "I read the Bible and I saw." [5]

An excellent observation. In planning his preaching program of evangelism, let the preacher read the Bible; there he will "see" how to do it. Not that he should copy and memorize and repeat in a wooden and mechanical way the message as Peter preached it. No. But the great fundamental truths, the mighty acts of God, the age-long unfolding purpose, the emphatic command that grows out of the magnificent truths found there—these are notes that need to be sounded as loudly in the twentieth century as in the first century.

Or take another approach toward the content of evangelistic preaching. John Wesley said: "I offered Christ to the people." The business of evangelistic preaching is to make the same offer.

In his book *The Practice of Evangelism*, Bryan Green says that the main content of evangelistic preaching should be the story of Christ. "The Father has given us the Son to be the bridge by which we can pass over into reconciliation with Himself; therefore show the people the bridge. It is more important to preach Christ than it is to preach about conversion, or even the need for conversion." [6]

"Preaching Christ" means far more than using the word Christ very often in your sermons. It does not mean proclaiming one phase of Christ's work to the exclusion of all other phases, nor does telling the story of Christ mean simply telling the stories about Christ. It means, rather, the proclamation of God's mighty deed in giving Christ to the world.

In telling of the mighty acts of God in Christ for man's redemption, one needs to give the story in two parts. On one side there are the plain, historical facts about Jesus of Nazareth whom God made both Lord and Christ. That may be a familiar story to the preacher, but let him not be fooled; it is not a familiar story to the average audience. The story needs to be told faithfully, carefully, but with great skill and all the dedicated art the preacher can muster. It is a story which, when told well, will charm and still an audience as few stories can.

But facts alone are not enough in telling the story of Jesus Christ. Facts are the beginning point, but we must go beyond the facts to their *interpretation*. What do the facts mean?

It is not enough to tell, no matter how forcefully, of Christ's death on the cross. Many men died on crosses. A man was crucified on the right and a man was crucified on the left of Jesus. Three crosses and as many deaths. What was the purpose, the intent, and the end of Christ's crucifixion? The resurrection? What does it mean? How does it relate to me? Does it mean the death of sin and the death of death? Does it mean that good is more powerful than evil, and that God will have the last word? How? Why? In what way? Does it mean that life is significant and meaningful? It looked on that dark Friday as if the very opposite were true.

Dorothy Sayers, the mystery story writer, once said that it was difficult to see how any person could make those facts dull and un-interesting; she was ready to affirm that there was nothing in this world quite as exciting as the gospel story. Yet, somehow preachers do manage to make the story dull. And, when the people hear a dull sermon on the facts of the gospel and the interpretation of those facts, they somehow get the idea that the facts are dull and their meaning is unimportant. They are unable to distinguish between dull preaching and exciting events. That is understandable, but it is tragic.

English novelist G. B. Stern once said about the word humdrum that it seemed such a tragic word—the same old stories, the same old activities, the same old words, the same old faces, the same old foods, papers, books, pictures, and music—just "humdrum." Then she began thinking about how the word was made up. She saw "humdrum" as made up of two words, each in its own right an exciting and exhilarating word. In "hum" she saw things humming, on the move, going somewhere, getting things done, visiting exciting places, and being a part of exciting movements. Then she looked at the other word, "drum," and she thought of the beat of drums, the stirring of the blood, the calling of people to battle. She felt the surge of rushing blood and marching feet. Humdrum? Far from it!

There is, too, in effective evangelistic preaching, a place for the proclamation of the "mighty acts of God" in and through his body, the church. There is so much criticism, so much pessimism, so much talk of failure and defeat. What God has done in the lives of his people as they came together forming these "gathered communities" is a great and thrilling story—how each man spoke to his brother and every man said to his neighbor, "Be of good courage." They said of the early Christians that they outthought, outloved, and outdied the pagans. That is a story worth telling. It speaks of a great need of our day.

In the musical, *Camelot*, it had been Arthur's dream that if men would come together at a Round Table where there was no head and no foot, where all men would be equal, they could settle their differences and there would be no need for wars. His dream did not become a reality. On the eve of battle as the king talks to a young knight, the old dream is rekindled. The king dares to hope that even yet the dream may become a reality, perhaps through this young boy. He says to the boy:

> Every evening from December to December,
> Before you fall asleep upon your cot
> Remind yourself again of all the tales
> That you have heard of Camelot.
> Ask every man you meet if he has heard the story,
> Tell it loud and clear if he has not:
> That once there was a flaming whisp of glory,
> Called Camelot.[7]

Delineating the Characteristics

What about the characteristics of the evangelistic sermon? In addition to the suggestions already given, let these additional words be borne in mind. The evangelistic sermon must be grounded in Scripture. This does not necessarily mean expository sermons. Indeed, few great evangelistic pastors have relied to any extent on expository preaching. Their preaching has been saturated in the Bible.

Again, evangelistic preaching needs to be structured on sound and solid doctrine. It needs to draw on great and noble themes—themes that force hearers to heed the gospel message, themes that launch out into the deeps of God and do not always hug the shallows of emotion alone. Evangelistic preaching is aided in its purpose by the use of great, hauntingly beautiful texts—texts that grip the mind and stir the imagination and prod the conscience of the hearer, and do, in themselves, bring God's convicting Spirit to the people.

The messages need to be "popular" in style, using that much-abused word in its best sense. Recently Terrence O'Flaherty, television editor for one of the great daily newspapers, pointed out something about the tastes of the viewing public that is worth the preacher's attention. He said:

If anyone wonders where America's mass entertainment tastes lie, a quick look at the top television favorites will be revealing. They point clearly to the fact that we may have become a nation of city folk, but our humor is still in the country. Gomer Pyle, Andy Griffith, Beverly Hillbillies, Red Skelton, Petticoat Junction, Green Acres, Jimmie Dean.

He goes on to point out that this is nothing new. He says that while now and then something will catch the attention of the country for a time, like the Beatles, rock 'n roll, the spies, and the witches, over the long haul there is nothing so successful as the country tune and no character so loved as the innocent hayseed. He concludes: "I suspect there is also a deeper reason for the attraction of this sort of entertainment. It is the basic American desire for a decent family show—one that is free of sex, sadism, psychiatry and sordidness, which have become the four horsemen of Hollywood's entertainment Apocalypse. The rural attraction may be corny, but it's clean." [8]

Pierce Harris, noted Methodist preacher and columnist, pushes the same button in a recent article in the *Atlanta Journal*. In his lead he says: "You are never going to overflow a sanctuary and send people away wanting to be different and better by a tiresome theological treatment of "the theory of transubstantiation." He adds that he "does not mind someone going away from his church saying, 'I do not agree with him,' but I do not want anybody, even a child, going away saying, 'I didn't understand him.'" [9]

There is no contradiction in what O'Flaherty and Harris say and what was stated about using great themes and structuring sermons along the lines of great doctrines. Consider the preaching and teaching of Jesus. No one, not even a child, would have gone away saying, "I do not understand." Yet the greatest and wisest had a feeling that they were unable to probe the depths of his words.

The titles of sermons need to be attractive. Remember that often the only pre-Sunday advertising for the message is its title tacked up on the bulletin board, printed in the Saturday paper, or noted in the mailed out bulletin. If the title does not make the outsider want to hear the sermon, it may keep him away from the sermon. A man may be present to hear the sermon and not be helped by it; he will not be helped by it if he does not hear it.

Consider the following titles, gleaned from many places:

From Rags to Riches
On Looking for a Kingdom
Know Your Heart's Condition
The Most Unforgettable Person
  I Know
Soul Erosion
The Best Things Are Not Free
Songs in the Night
How to Become a Christian
What Christ Does for Men
How to Take God's Help
How to Trust God's Care
What Is Right with the
  Church?
This Life Is Worth Living
God and Man's Need
Begin Living Today
Why Not Try Christ's Way?
The Recoil of Repudiated
  Responsibilities
Facing Failure with Faith
When Life Tumbles In, What
  Then?

The Comfort and Challenge of
  Christianity
A Good Word for Jesus Christ
All This and Heaven, Too
A Magnificent Obsession
When the Roll Is Called Down
  Here
We Sail Under Sealed Orders
On Going Back to Go Forward
What Are You Standing For?
What in the World Are You
  Doing for Heaven's Sake?
The Kind of Repentance that
  Does Some Good
Our God Is Able
The Naturalness of Faith
Impossible to Escape God
Learn to Be Alone Together
The Satisfaction of Living Your
  Life with God
Magnificent Reminders

How does one go about planning his preaching program according to the evangelistic emphasis? One way is to follow the Christian Year. Beginning with Christmas or the Advent season, a man may plan his preaching around the life and work of Jesus. He may deal with the great events in Jesus' life such as his appearance in the Temple when he was twelve, his baptism by John at the Jordan, his temptations in the wilderness, the beginning of his ministry in Galilee, and his call of the disciples.

Series and courses of sermons also offer abundant opportunity for proclaiming the evangelistic message. Think of a few of the possible series:

The Friends of Jesus
The Enemies of Jesus
Questions Jesus Asked
Questions Asked of Jesus
Questions Asked About Jesus
Names for the Followers of
  Jesus
Names for the Church

The Parables
The Miracles
Personal Evangelism Cases of
  Jesus
Conversations of Jesus
The Sermons of Jesus
Crises in the Life of Christ
The Prayers of Jesus

The techniques for setting forth the evangelistic plan are the same as those for other plans already discussed. I would only add two notes in conclusion: (1) All that has been said about the importance of reading God's Word publicly is applicable here. (2) This plan may be used in every service, in only one service, or only in both Sunday services. This plan offers a wide range of choices for the pastor to use at his discretion.

MAY, YEAR

	Event	A.M.	P.M.	Wed.
1st Week	3rd Sunday after Easter Christian Home Week B National Family Week	**Names Used For The Followers of Christ** "They Were Called: 'Believers' " Scripture Lessons: Deut. 10:12-22 Rom. 8:18-25 Text: Acts 5:12-14	You And Your Relationship to God "How To Trust God's Care" Scripture Lesson: Psalm 55:16-22 Text: Psalm 55:22	**Questions Jesus Asked** "How Is It That Ye Sought Me?" Scripture Lesson: Luke 2:40-50
2nd Week	4th Sunday after Easter Festival of the Christian Home B Mother's Day Girls' Auxiliary Focus Week B Rural Life Sunday	"They Were Called: 'Disciples' " Scripture Lessons: Deut. 11:18-21 Matt. 11:28-30 Text: Acts 6:7	"How To Believe In God's Love" Scripture Lesson: Rom. 5:1-8 Text: Rom. 5:5	"Why Are Ye Fearful?" Scripture Lesson: Mark 4:35-41
3rd Week	5th Sunday after Easter Aldersgate Sunday M Radio & Television Sunday B	"They Were Called: 'Brothers' " Scripture Lessons: Gen. 15:1-6 Heb. 13:1-6 Text: 1 John 3:14	"How To Take God's Help" Scripture Lesson: Eph. 3:14-21 Text: Eph. 3:20	"Wouldest Thou Be Made Whole?" Scripture Lesson: John 5:1-9
4th Week	6th Sunday after Easter	"They Were Called: 'Those of the Way' " Scripture Lessons: 2 Kings 5:1-14 Eph. 2:4-10 Text: Acts 9:2	"How To Find God's Will" Scripture Lesson: Matt. 26:36-46 Text: Matt. 26:39	"Sayest Thou This of Thyself?" Scripture Lesson: John 18:28-34
5th Week	7th Sunday after Easter Whitsunday, Pentecost Memorial Day	"They Were Called: 'Christians' " Scripture Lessons: Dan. 6:4-10 Phil. 3:17-21 Text: Acts 11:25-26	"How To Draw On God's Resources" Scripture Lesson: Phil. 4:1-13 Text: Phil. 4:13	

11

Baptism and the Lord's Supper

(PLAN VII)

From the earliest days of the churches the ordinances of baptism and the Lord's Supper have been observed. There was no question about their place in the life of the believing band. Before the New Testament had been written, before there was a church house in existence, before there was an accepted creed or formulated doctrine, before there was a pope in Rome or a bishop in Constantinople, the ordinances existed. Professor John S. Whale has said:

These rites of Baptism and Eucharist go back to Christ himself. There is nothing older than this in Christendom . . . This is the earliest Gospel. Indeed it is rooted in the immemorial covenant which God made with his people Israel. We take Bread and we take the Cup because the Redeemer himself is the fountainhead of this living tradition.[1]

The ordinances are not only ancient in origin; their observance by the churches has been continuous. From the plain and simple services observed in homes to the secretive meetings in the catacombs to the elaborate and colorful services held in the great cathedrals, the observance has continued. Some parts of the simple ceremony used in New Testament times have been eliminated; many items and customs have been added. But the ordinances have been continuous. In spite of wide and various interpretations, controversy and doctrinal disputes, theological debates and ecclesiastical councils, names and designations, the followers of Christ have observed these ordinances.

In their observance the churches have placed the ordinances at the center of life and worship. This has been true not only for the Roman Catholic with his High Mass, it has also been true for the Calvinist with his insistence upon the Scriptures as the fountainhead of his authority. Calvin maintained that two things faithfully done made the church: the preaching of the Word of God, and the administration of the sacraments.

Nor have modern theologians been any less insistent upon the central place of this part of worship. Listen to Emil Brunner:

The Sacraments are the divinely given flying buttresses which save the Church from collapse. In how many of the churches today do we not find the Sacraments almost the sole biblical footing—the only biblical element that has been able to withstand the caprices of the gifted minister who lives by his own wisdom rather than for the Scriptures. Even the most audacious minister has not dared lay hands on the Sacraments. And they are what they are! One may so interpret the words of Scripture that the words speak the opposite of their intent; but the Sacraments, thank God, speak a language independent of the language of the pastor. They are a part of the church least affected by theological or other tendencies; and that is their special blessing.[2]

A large portion of Christendom has consistently believed that the minimum basis on which a church could rightly be called a Christian church was when it proclaimed the Word of God and when it observed these two rites, baptism and the Lord's Supper. A large portion of the churches has believed just as firmly that these two rites represented the maximum expression of the church—not its sole expression, but its maximum expression; not the proclamation of the "works of the church," but the proclamation of the "works of the Lord of the church"; not what man has done or must do, but what God in Christ has done, continues to do, and shall be doing forever. This is what makes the church the church. In this faith millions have lived and millions have died. They have believed that the entire and complete redeeming mission of Christ was "set forth" when the Word of God was preached and when it was *seen*.

In the clear light of the Scriptures and a rightful understanding of church history, no one may take lightly the place and significance of baptism and the Lord's Supper. For, as Harold E. Fey has said,

> Once a church which possessed no paid ministry, no priesthood, no cathedrals or church buildings, no endowments, no salaried bishops or secretaries, no publicity except the lies told by its enemies, held a disintegrating world together and laid the basis of a new civilization. Its power was not its own. What it had was a gift. The gift was given it in meetings of little groups who assembled before dawn in houses on back streets and in caves under Rome . . . whenever they met they broke bread with gladness and singleness of heart and shared the cup of their covenant with Christ.[3]

This is a book on planning your preaching. Its intent is not primarily doctrinal and theological. Therefore, it spends little time in affirming or in denying particular views and interpretations of the meaning of baptism and the Lord's Supper. The purpose of this chapter is to emphasize the importance of these ordinances in any worthy preaching plan. It is impossible to deal with the subject effectively, to make use of helpful literature in the field, without using certain words and terms that would not be entirely acceptable by any single Christian group. It should not be assumed that because certain words and terms appear in the discussion that the writer himself approves of each.

For example, the words "sacrament" and "ordinance" have already appeared again and again. Each word has an interesting history; the two words certainly do not mean the same. Most of the "freer churches" use the word "ordinance" rather than "sacrament." There is good cause for this. As the word sacrament is often understood, it represents a position that these groups do not espouse. Yet, one of the basic and original meanings of the word "sacrament" derives from the oath that the Roman soldier gave to his emperor when he entered the service of his country. Few Christians, whatever their denominational affiliation or doctrinal position, would find this meaning objectionable since every faithful Christian gladly gives his oath of allegiance to Jesus Christ.

The Scriptures do not lay down guidelines for the frequency

with which the ordinances will be observed. This is a matter that is usually decided by the particular communion and the individual churches of that communion. Some groups baptize only once each year, regardless of numbers. Other churches have a tradition of baptizing every week. Some denominations observe the Lord's Supper weekly, some observe it monthly, quarterly, biannually, or only annually. Whatever the plan, and circumstances will usually alter the plan, there needs to be a plan for preaching on the great truths set forth by these ordinances.

If there is no planned program of preaching, one of several things will result. There will be no solid teaching and proclamation of the truths contained in the ordinances, or the preaching that is done will be haphazard, a few truths repeated over and over while other great teachings will be ignored entirely. The doctrines contained in these ordinances are too great and varied to be dealt with adequately in one or in a dozen messages. Only in a carefully planned program of preaching over the year can the minister instruct his people adequately.

There is much to be said for planning the preaching so that the sermons do not come on the hour when the ordinance is being observed. One reason is that if the ordinance is given the place in the hour of worship that it deserves, there will be little time for the sermon. Too, the people may be able to give more objective hearing to the sermon at a time when they are not immediately and personally involved in the event.

Again, there is the matter of instruction. While the minister will want to deal positively with the ordinances in his preaching, there will be times when he feels it necessary to point out error as well as truth. On the whole it is better for the great affirmations to be proclaimed at the time of the observance. Let the people at those high hours be reminded of the "mighty works of God" rather than of the erroneous beliefs of men.

Baptizing Them

The devil, no less than God, was very real to Martin Luther. The familiar story of Luther's hurling a bottle of ink at his satanic majesty bears out the statement. Other incidents indicate the condition. Luther had his hours of doubt and despair. In such hours he would face himself and the tempter with the words, "Baptizatus sum, baptizatus sum"—"I have been baptized, I have been baptized." As that event was brought to his mind, that decisive act of commitment and of dedication reviewed, he would experience the renewal of courage and of hope and of faith.

Tertullian, one of the church fathers, tells in his *Confessions* what a happy occasion the baptismal experience was in the early days. He says that it took place on one of the great festive days of the church, usually on Easter. Those who were to be baptized had been instructed in the Christian faith and had memorized the material given them, including the Lord's Prayer. They were dressed in white robes, then were baptized "in the name of the Father and of the Son and of the Holy Ghost." Every step in the procedure was one of joy and triumph, for it signified the entrance into a new life, a life in Christ, and into the body of Christ.

Surely, the average service of baptism would be helped by something of that triumphant note. In the early pioneer days of our country it was easier, it would seem, to experience the note of joy and triumph. The services were held in the great out-of-doors, by a stream or lake. Nature was awake with beauty; flowers, birds, bright sun were in evidence; friends were standing by in bright garments; glad voices were lifted in song. The very setting seemed to make its contribution to the joyous occasion.

In contrast, consider the average service today. There is no denying that the service held within the churches is more convenient; it can be held at any season of the year. Few would want to dispense with this convenience. Still, the baptistry is often inadequate in size, lighting, entrance, exit, and cleanliness. The dressing rooms—if they exist—are inadequate in size, equipment, and cleanliness. The garments worn are far from being attractive and comfortable. The ordinance is "tacked on" at the close of a full service, or it is rushed in at the beginning of the service. There is not adequate time for explanation and interpretation to the candidates. Often the entire service adds up to an unsatisfactory and unsatisfying experience for all, especially for the persons being baptized.

Teaching Them

The ordinance of baptism is seldom explained or expounded by the present-day minister. It is assumed that the candidate and the congregation know the significance of the ordinance. Such is not the case. The only bit of knowledge one can safely assume that the candidate and the congregation understand is the *form* of baptism that the particular church practices. Important, yes, but if this is all that matters, the church might be blood brother to the man who rejoiced when his doctor told him that he had stomach ulcers. "Why doctor," he exclaimed, "That is a lucky break for me; I was afraid I had something that would show." Often what does not show is as dangerous (or as rewarding) as what is seen. That is true in baptism no less than in medicine.

The minister needs to instruct his people in the meaning of baptism. However, when he comes to look for literature and other helps on the subject, he may be disappointed. There are few helps. It has been estimated that there are a hundred books on the Lord's Supper for every one on baptism. Strange. A proper understanding of baptism is involved in the entire evangelistic task of the church. When the ordinance is appropriately and meaningfully observed, it proclaims "the whole wide world for Jesus." It is difficult to see how any minister could more forcefully declare the great doctrines of salvation than to give this ordinance its meaningful place. Let him be very sure that his people and, as far as his ability makes possible, the world understand the meaning.

Consider the wealth of sermon topics in this area. First, there are the *implications* of baptism. Some of these points the thoughtful minister will declare with ringing faith, some he will seek to clarify, some he may wish to place question marks over. But, each is an implication that needs his attention, and on each his people need instruction. Each is worthy of a sermon, in some cases a series of sermons.

Baptism symbolizes a new life. It speaks of death to sin. It de-

clares for resurrection "in Christ." It speaks of burial to unrighteous-
ness and of living unto righteousness. Here is a place for the
thoughtful minister to reintroduce, to acquaint his people with some
great theological words: atonement, regeneration, conversion,
purification, cleansing, renewal, the new birth, sanctification, vicari-
ous, Law, grace, wrath of God, love of God, and mercy of God.
All are significant areas for preaching in relation to baptism. If
these words and concepts are dealt with meaningfully, sympathetically, interestingly, if they are interpreted in terms and thought
forms that the "average man" can comprehend, they can be
channels of dynamic preaching.

Second, consider the *responsibility* of baptism as a rich vein for
sermon mining. There is the responsibility resting upon parents. A
parent cannot believe for his child; the responsibility for faith,
belief, acceptance of Jesus Christ is an individual, personal
responsibility. It cannot be transferred or assumed by proxy.

Yet, there is a real sense in which the parent cannot avoid believing for the child. The parent believes or disbelieves; he does
this in sight of the child. There is no way the parent can avoid this
responsibility, for his example, influence, evaluations, and decisions
register upon the child. It is as if the loving Father said to every
father and mother: "You have become fellow-creators with me; I
entrust into your care the life and destiny of this child; take him
and raise him for me; I shall hold you responsible. Be assured,
and never forget, that you must face the question, 'Is it well with
the child?' "

There are few more relevant places to preach the parents'
responsibility than through sermons on baptism. Just as the responsibility for Christian commitment rests upon the individual and
cannot be assumed by proxy on the part of another, just so the home
has a responsibility for Christian faith, Christian nurture, Christian
education that cannot be assumed by the church, the school, the
community, or the state.

Think of the responsibility that baptism places upon the church.
Just as the parents are forced to assume a responsibility for the
child, so the church is required to assume a responsibility for the

baptized. Christian baptism is the doorway into the believing community; baptism takes place at the request of and by the permission of and on the authority of the church. It takes place within the loving bonds of the church. John Donne wrote: "When the church baptizes a child, that action concerns me, for the child is thereby connected to that which is my head too, and ingrafted into that body whereof I am a member."

Just as the newly baptized is required to make certain commitments and to assume certain obligations, so the church makes certain commitments to the baptized and assumes certain obligations to and for him. The baptized comes into a new family relationship, a family relationship of concern and caring. In a vital sense the church says to the baptized child, whether young or old, what Moses said to Hobab: "We are journeying unto the place of which the Lord said, I will give it you: come thou with us, and we will do thee good: for the Lord hath spoken good concerning Israel. . . . And it shall be, if thou go with us, yea, it shall be, that what goodness the Lord shall do unto us, the same will we do unto thee." (Num. 10:29–32).

The church assumes a responsibility for education and for nurture, for truth and for virtue. It must see that the atmosphere and the influence of the church is Christian; it must see that the educational program, in content and in methods, is worthy. It must, as far as is possible, see that the baptized increase in wisdom and in stature and in favor with God and with men.

Once Stephen Leacock, author and humorist, found himself in church without his purse. When the offering plates were passed, he quickly tore a flyleaf from his prayer book and wrote on it, "I.O.U. $2.50," and put the note in the collection plate. It would be just as reasonable for the church to hand every person it baptizes an "I.O.U." note, for it does assume obligations for that individual.

There is, too, the obligation that the newly baptized disciple assumes toward Christ and toward his body, the church. The baptized must never be allowed to believe that baptism bestows

blessings and privileges without leveling obligations and responsibilities. The order is exceedingly important: first, the indicative,
then the imperative. First, let the new Christian know what God
in Christ has done and will continue to do for him; then, on the
basis of the mighty and gracious acts of God, the Christian must
respond in loving obedience and in willing service. His obedience
and service are in the name of Jesus Christ, but his obedience and
service are given in the context of and in cooperation with the
church. He is now a member of the body of Christ and he must so
live and act.

There is a third area for preaching on baptism that the minister
should never fail to emphasize. This is the area of the promises of
God. Paul wrote to the Corinthians: "the Son of God, Jesus Christ,
whom we preached among you, Silvanus and Timothy and I, was
not Yes and No; but in him it is always Yes. For all the promises of
God find their Yes in him" (2 Cor. 1:19-20, RSV). Those
promises are never more evident, never more in need of proclamation than in relationship to baptism. The candidate is baptized in
"the name of the Father, and of the Son, and of the Holy Spirit."
That says many things. One unmistakable thing it says is this: This
is not man's doing but God's. The plan is God's; the initiative is
God's; the gift is God's; the resources are God's; the glory is God's.
Here, if anywhere, he is "the Alpha and the Omega": the beginning
of all that baptism signifies, and the end of all that baptism in-
volves.

Lyman Abbott, the New England clergyman, wrote a version
of the Model Prayer that shows in dramatic form what faith in the
promises of God means. He wrote the prayer this way: "Our
Brethren who are on the earth, Hallowed be our name. Our Kingdom come, Our will be done, for there is no heaven. We must get
this day our daily bread; We neither forgive nor are forgiven. We
fear no temptation, for we deliver ourselves from evil. For ours is
the kingdom and the power, for there is no glory and no forever." [4]
Let the minister preach the promises of God in relation to the
ordinance of baptism.

As Oft As You Do It

The Christian churches have given far more attention to the Lord's Supper, as stated earlier, than they have to baptism. This is difficult to understand and the disproportionate emphasis may be regretted. However, no intelligent follower of Christ will regret any true emphasis upon the Communion, for, indeed, it is doubtful that too much emphasis could be placed upon it, provided the interpretation is a true one. Hugh Thompson Kerr's statement is valid: "The sacrament of the Lord's Supper holds in its keeping, in its words, in its symbolism, in its administration, the very substance of the Christian faith. It does not reflect the thought of the age, or of any age, but speaks of 'the Lamb of God, that taketh away the sin of the world.'" [5]

While much attention has been given to the ordinance, and while there is no lack of literature upon the subject, the fact remains that there is a great need for solid preaching on the theme. If this preaching is to be whole, valid, and significant to the hearer, it will have to be taken into an overall planned preaching program. Otherwise, as in the case of preaching on baptism, the emphasis will be partial and haphazard.

A different situation exists for those churches that celebrate the Lord's Supper every Sunday from those who celebrate it less frequently. Again, much may be said for the major portion of the preaching being done on Sundays when the ordinance is not observed. The same reasons prevail as stated earlier. But, if the ordinance is observed each Sunday, obviously this cannot be done.

In many of the churches a great deal more thought needs to be given to the actual administration of the service than is usually the case. Often the service is handled clumsily. The minister, as well as those assisting him, seem to be in doubt as to the order of procedure. Paul's words that all things must be done "decently and in order" need to be heard. There is no excuse for the service's not being conducted with simplicity, beauty, and dignity. The relevance of the service does not depend upon aesthetics, but neither is the service aided by ugliness and clumsiness. There is the story of the old mountaineer who interrupted the learned speaker with

the words: "Brother, the Lord can git 'long without yar larnin'."
"Yes," was the response, "and he can get along without your
ignorance, too."

One of the fruitful sources of preaching on the Lord's Supper
resides in the different *names* that are used for the ordinance. Often
emphasis has been placed upon the different *meanings* of the
ordinance. The two sources are close neighbors; if you are on good
terms with one you will not be unacquainted with the other. Some
of the names may be dealt with by scholars in a strong and positive
way, while some will be handled in a questioning or negative
way. But, each will have grist for the resourceful preacher's mill
and his people will find the bread nourishing.

The *Lord's Supper* is one of the names by which the ordinance
is most universally known and most greatly loved. Speak the
words anywhere in the Protestant world and the heart comes to
attention and the affection kneels. It speaks of the Saviour, of his
presence, of his blessing of the bread and the cup. He is still the
host who sits at the head of the table, and there is a promise that as
he breaks the bread we shall recognize him. The name suggests, in
the words of the lovely spiritual, "Let us break bread together on
our knees." Paul uses the words in 1 Corinthians 11:20, and in
1 Corinthians 10:21 he calls it "the table of the Lord."

It is also called the *Communion*. Again, it is Paul who uses the
words in 1 Corinthians 10:16–17. He says: "The cup of blessing
which we bless, is it not the communion of the blood of Christ?
The bread which we break, is it not the communion of the body of
Christ? For we being many are one bread, and one body." The
word is the Greek word "koinōnia;" it means fellowship, partaker,
common. It means sharing together the service. It suggests that
the believer does not partake of the elements alone but in fellowship with Christ. The term also suggests the relationship of fellow
disciples, for from the first night in the upper room it has been the
means of a reaffirmation of the ties among the followers of Jesus.
It is a church ordinance, not an exercise for lone and individual
Christians.

The *Eucharist* is an ancient and honored title taken from the

Greek and meaning "thanksgiving." The word appears as early as the ordinance appears. "He took the cup, and gave *thanks*"; "He took the cup, and when he had given *thanks*." "Grace" and "gratitude" come from the same root. Sometimes it is felt that the word is associated with a particular interpretation of the meal, such as is practiced by the Roman Catholic Church. This is not the case. It is simply one of the early terms used for the ordinance and is meant to show that the meal was blessed by the Saviour.

The ordinance is called the *Mass*. This is the term that the Roman Catholic Church uses for the entire service. *Mass* comes from the Latin word *mittere*, meaning to send. It came about through the custom of dismissing at a certain point in the service all who were not baptized believers. The term does not appear until the third century, so, unlike the other names so far used, it does not appear in the Scriptures.

The service is also called the *Passover*. Paul says, "Christ our passover is sacrificed for us" (1 Cor. 5:7). The name is, of course, associated with the Passover of the Jews' deliverance from Egypt. The Christian is not delivered from Egyptian bondage but from the bondage of sin and of death. Therefore, the Christian life is a festive life, a life of freedom and deliverance. In the offering of the sacrifice of Christ, in the association of life with him, the covenant is signed; the promises are given.

The Armenian churches call the ordinance the *Oblation*. (Certain parts of the Roman service also bear this name). Under this term the service is thought of as an offering to God—something that the celebrant does for God but on man's behalf. God has to be appeased; so, by offering this sacrifice in the form of the elements, God is propitiated. Even in this extreme view, there is an element of truth that the Protestant Christian can gladly affirm and to which he can joyously subscribe. It is not by the disciple's own merit that he stands before God, but in and through the righteousness of Christ Jesus.

In the early church the ordinance was called agapé, or "love feast." This term included the fellowship meal and the Lord's Supper, which was, of course, natural since both were served in the "house churches" and were almost always observed concurrently. There is something appealing about the title. Surely, the present-day church would have much to gain from a realization that every worthy observance of the Lord's Supper is of necessity a love feast—a love feast of the individual with his Lord and Saviour, and through that relationship a love feast with his fellow believers.

The *breaking of bread* is a biblical term often used for the ordinance today. It sustains the tender memories of how Christ broke the bread and gave it to the disciples, and his command that they were to observe the custom until he came again.

These eight names are the most prominent designations by which the ordinance is known. The wise and resourceful minister will find in a careful study of them much food for his own soul, and much worthy preaching for his people. He will, by wise and careful use of them, have a more intelligent and well-anchored congregation.

What's in a Name?

The listing of a few selected titles that ministers have used for their sermons on the Lord's Supper will suggest something of the richness that awaits the minister who carefully plans his preaching.

The Place Where We May Well Be at One
The Fellowship of Kindred Minds
The Common Table
The Meaning of the Lord's Supper
The Bread of the Upper Room
Let Us Break Bread Together on Our Knees
The Apprehended Presence
The Owner's Mark
Whose Name Do You Bear?
Your New Name
Who Shall Separate Us
Reclaiming Our Heritage

Rejoice, Ye Pure in Heart
The King of Love My Shepherd Is
The Church's One Foundation
Crown Him with Many Crowns
Spirit of God, Descend upon My Heart
Jesus, Thou Joy of Loving Hearts
Bread of the World in Mercy Broken
According to Thy Gracious Word
The Power of the Symbolic
The Brotherhood of the Burning Heart

Personal Involvement
Received and Delivered
Anthem of Emancipation
Get Rid of Yourselves
According to Thy Gracious
    Words
Here, O My Lord, I See Thee
    Face to Face
O Jesus, I Have Promised
Saviour! Thy Dying Love
Guests of God
The Cost of Communion
The King's Table
The King's Cupbearer
Light from the Upper Room
This Do in Remembrance of
    Me
God's Action—and Ours

The Heart's Preparation
More Than Memorial
The Original Intent
The Nature of the Fellowship
The Spell of the Cross
The Guestchamber
Thou Preparest a Table
    Before Me
Sacrifice and Song
Comrades of the Gathered
    Community
The Relevance of the Upper
    Room
Life's Upper Rooms
Will He Come to the Feast?
The Consecration of the
    Commonplace

Let this chapter on the ordinances end with some words written by a noted biographer in an entirely different context. Emil Ludwig, biographer of Napoleon, Bismarck, and Goethe among others, wrote: "If you are to write a biography of a man, you must think with him and eat with him. You cannot make a person live in the mind of another unless you have a furious, mad, passionate relationship with him." [6]

It would be difficult to find words that more nearly mirror the need every minister has who would portray to his people the significance of baptism and the Lord's Supper.

12

A Tower on
the Weekly Journey

(PLAN VIII)

The midweek service needs to be included in the minister's over all preaching plans and integrated closely into the body of his teaching ministry. It is one of the regularly scheduled services of the church. This between-Sundays meeting is attended by two groups within the church: (1) those present for the Sunday services, and (2) those, a smaller number, who cannot attend the Sunday services.

For the benefit of both groups, the midweek service needs to be included in the long-range preaching plans. It needs to be included for the benefit of those who attend the regular services of worship, lest there be too much repetition and the service make no real contribution to the people's spiritual, intellectual, social, and moral growth. The service needs to be included in the long-range plans for the benefit of those who do not attend the regular Sunday services, or it may be left out of the major emphasis and the great spiritual currents of the church's teaching and proclamation.

There is another reason why the midweek service should be included in the long-range teaching and preaching plans. It, along with the hours of worship on Sunday, has "one Lord, one faith, one baptism, one God and Father of all, who is over all, and through all, and in you all." The Sunday and Wednesday services draw their resources from the same stream and move toward a common goal. Every argument that can be advanced in favor of a planned program of preaching and teaching for the services held in the church on Sunday is equally valid for the midweek service.

Names for the Service

"The midweek service"—that is the term being used. Why? Much has been written, spoken, and put into practice about a new name for this service. The ancient and honored name for it, of course, was "prayer meeting," or "the prayer meeting service," or "the hour of prayer." Those who no longer use one of these titles give various reasons for not doing so.

It is said that the name "prayer meeting" should apply to all the services, not just to one—that there is no more actual praying done at this service than at other services. The old title indicates, some say, a type of service that can no longer be experienced; for better or for worse, the name now has a connotation that is not attractive. It tends to limit the type of service that is needed. Prayer, yes, but much more than prayer is needed. Whether you agree or not, it may be that a change in name is due.

The danger is, of course, in believing that when the name is changed, the quality of the service is automatically improved. This is not true. The lady said that like snow and peanuts, debt and gossip, the older she got the meaner she became! A service may become less and less vital the older it gets, regardless of the name it bears. It takes more than a name to guarantee a relevant service. Still, names are important.

Here are some of the names that have been and are being used to designate this between-Sundays service: Church Night, Family Night, The Fellowship Night, The Friendship Night, The Faith, Food and Fun Night, The Happy Night, The Glad Service, The Hour of Power, The Power to Become Hour, The Good News Hour, and The Secret Place Hour.

In many churches no name is used, for no service is held. In some cases this may be justified. There are difficulties faced by some churches is promoting a midweek service. These obstacles are not new today; they may be intensified. In 1916 Halford Luccock and Warren F. Cook wrote a little book called *The Mid-Week Service*. The first sentence in the book, written fifty years ago, reads: "Many

an inquest has been held over the prayer meeting." The authors
then proceeded to draw an analogy between the old story, "Who
Killed Cock Robin?" and "What killed the prayer meeting?" The
witnesses who came to the stand to bear their testimony as to
"what killed the prayer meeting" might give the same testimony
today, and scarcely a word would need to be changed.

If there are no new arguments against the midweek service,
there are some new arguments for it. *There are some new needs
for the service and there are some new doors of opportunity open
to it.* The needs cannot be met, the doors cannot be entered
effectively without long-range planning. The first of these open
doors—call it a need, call it an opportunity, call it a problem—results
from the transient membership that makes up our churches.

Ralph Sockman used to explain why the Methodists did not move
their ministers as often as they once did. He said that it used to be
necessary to change the ministers because the congregation remained the same, but now it was unnecessary to move the ministers
because the congregation was constantly moving. The central core
of leadership remains fairly stable in many churches, but not always. In certain areas where the space program, nuclear development, and military effort are strong, churches have been healthy
one week and nonexistent the next. Like the Arabs, those who made
up the membership folded their tents in the night and were on the
move.

In such situations the words of Jesus are pertinent: "What thou
doest, do quickly." Now, even in small congregations, it is possible
to attend Sunday morning worship for months and not get to know
anyone—really get to know them—other than by name. It is in the
family atmosphere, the give and take, the dialogue of a midweek
service that one quickly gets to know individuals. It is there that
voices are heard, attitudes are discerned, kinships are established,
mutual tasks and learning experiences are entered.

A second pressing need for the midweek service in today's
world is made evident in the work habits of the people. More
industries, factories, shops, stores, even farms, are on a twenty-four-

hour, seven-day-week schedule than ever before. The pattern may be deplored; it cannot be denied, and it must be dealt with creatively.

A few churches are trying. Services are being held at different times, in different places, and with different formats. Chapels are being built or improvised near factories. The periods of worship parallel the night and day work shifts. An attempt is made to conduct services that are brief and relevant to the immediate needs of the workers. This is all to the good. There is nothing particularly sacred about eleven o'clock on Sunday morning as the hour for worship.

The Gathered Community

But there is something important about the church, the body of Christ, coming together as the body of Christ for the purpose of worship. Improvised places of worship, services held at different times of day and night for a particular group of people, brought together to that place at that time by employment requirements, may supplement but never take the place of the "gathered community." This community is characterized by different ages, sexes, interests, vocations, neighborhoods, and cultures, brought together voluntarily for the purpose of worship and nurture. Let the people voluntarily enter into covenant with one another, let them come together in a place that their own loving gifts and service have made possible, and a plus will be experienced that cannot be supplied by the industrialized and specialized chapel idea.

It is at this point that the midweek service can play an increasingly vital role. There will be those who can meet in the churches as a part of the body of Christ between Sundays who cannot meet there on the Lord's Day; their work responsibilities will not allow it. At another time—six months, twelve months, five years later—they may be able to meet with their fellow members on Sunday morning and evening. In the meantime, the spiritual needs of these individuals should be met and an opportunity provided where they can make their contribution to and through the church. Let the midweek service, then, take its place as a full-fledged colleague in the task of proclaiming, teaching, and nurturing.

There is a third opportunity open to the midweek service that is more evident today than it was in the past. This opportunity is suggested by the considerations above, but it has not been spelled out. It is the opportunity to meet the needs of different groups within the membership of the church, and/or the opportunity to meet different needs of the same group within the membership of the church in different ways.

Rapid shifts in population, swift urbanization, the mushrooming of industrial areas formerly agricultural in makeup, the great influx of military personnel—all of this makes for a type of membership in our churches that is different from anything known in the past.

Propelled by these and other causes, members of our churches come from widely different backgrounds; they come from large and small churches, from town and city churches, from churches that have formal services of worship and from churches that know a very simple and informal type of service; they come from churches that have great robed choirs under professional guidance; and they come from churches that have none of these advantages.

There is no one type of setting and form of service that God honors above all others. Men have found God and his will for their lives in many different types of services. If the same group of people could stay together in the same church for a sufficient length of time, they could—through love, patience, understanding, and education—be led to worship meaningfully through any one type of approach. However, as stated above, many of these people will be moving on to other communities, churches, and centers of service before this orientation can take place. What then? Within reason, the churches should minister to the different groups in words, forms and symbols that are meaningful and comfortable for the spirits of these differing groups.

The midweek service can make a vital contribution at this point. There is one gospel and there is one Bible. But, just as that one gospel, using that one Bible, is presented differently in the Sunday School class from the way it is presented in the pulpit on Sunday morning, so it can be presented differently on Wednesday evening. Generally, it can be presented more informally; there can be more of the intimate family atmosphere. This approach more nearly resembles the approach to worship that many individuals have known and without which they find it difficult to feel at home.

It needs to be said, too, that this type of service makes a contribution to a wider group than just those who come from the less sophisticated backgrounds. It meets a certain need in the life of every worshiper, no matter how strict, formal, and liturgical he likes his worship. The Christian church began in the home. The sentence, "Greet the church that meets in thy house," is often seen. There was probably not a church house in existence when the last of the New Testament books were written. The best-loved words and phrases of our faith come to us with the flavor and coloring of the family: father, brother, elder brother, family, household, household of faith, inheritance, family of God.

If the closeness and dearness of these early experiences are to endure, there must be some place where the cultivation of sympathy, concern, fellowship, joy, and mutual self-giving may be known. Many churches are so large that it is extremely difficult for them to know this quality and type of Christian life. The Wednesday evening hour of worship offers one of the best opportunities. The need cannot be adequately met through the Sunday School class or other types of organizations within the church; the need can be met only within the context of the church itself. A good case could be made for the statement that the midweek service may be the time when the church, ideally, is more nearly the "family of God" than at any other time in the week.

Cumulative Effect

A fourth opportunity for the midweek service, an opportunity that is not unique to the present day but is reemphasized by the needs of the present day, lies in the area of accumulation. The minister needs to be reminded repeatedly that his work in proclaim-

ing and teaching has this cumulative quality about it. It is possible
for the minister to place too great an importance upon a single service as that service relates to his overall ministry. It is easy for the
minister to feel that his success or failure depends largely upon his
ability or lack of ability to communicate effectively with everyone
in his audience at each service.

Of course, this is incorrect. The impact of the gospel cannot be
gauged by the results of one service. It has to be measured over a
much longer period of time with many different types of services
considered.

The minister's concern should be at another point. He should
put forth conscientious effort to make sure that every service bears
witness to the gospel. He should be sure that the different services
are also linked with one another in an overall, long-range plan. If
these two requirements are met, the minister need not be over-
anxious about the effect of any one single service.

When the minister includes the midweek service in his overall
plan for teaching and preaching, different approaches will be used.
At times the emphasis may be the same as that in the Sunday services, parallel to it, or complementary. At other times the emphasis
in the middle service should be in contrast to the other services.

Whatever the approach, two things should characterize the
Wednesday service: (1) It should be a vital part of an overall plan;
and (2) each service, whenever it is held, should have a certain
completeness about it. The old-fashioned Saturday serial where,
along with the heroine, the viewers were often left hanging in space
has no place in a midweek service. This does not contradict what
has been said about the cumulative quality of the services. There
is the main plot and there are contributing episodes, each of which
has a certain independence. Each episode makes a contribution to
the plot, but the story is never complete until all the episodes have
been added.

Consider a few examples of how the midweek service may be
tied into the minister's long-range plan. He has planned his
preaching according to the Christian Year and it is the Advent
season. Four Sundays are included in the season; each Sunday has

a different emphasis: the Creation, the Bible, the Prophets, and
the Forerunner. A few questions will point up ways that the midweek services during this season may make their contribution to
the whole picture.

What does Advent mean? What is its significance for today?
When and how and where did its observance begin? What are
some of the different ways that it has been observed? Why do
many churches not observe it? How may the emphasis of Advent
that is made in church be amplified in the home, the school, at
work, at play, by individuals, and by groups? What are some
appropriate materials to use in the observance of Advent—materials
from the realms of music, art, poetry, novel, drama, as well as the
Scriptures?

Simply to ask such questions suggests background, supplemen-
tary, educational approaches for a series of midweek services that
would be relevant within themselves, and yet make their contribution to the overall preaching program for the season.

Or, the season is Epiphany. The emphasis is manifestation—how
God has manifested his love for sinful men and nations. The
season of Epiphany runs into February. February is the month
of the "birthdays of the great." We are familiar with the birthdays of
Washington, Lincoln, and St. Valentine; there are birthdays of
other great men in February, including Ruskin and Longfellow.
One way that God has manifested his love and power is through
the lives of great and good men. Along with a solid, doctrinal
preaching program on Sunday, plan a dynamic series of biographical studies on Wednesday evenings of men and women whom God
has used and how he has used them.

If the history of the local church is a long one, and if that history
has been preserved, the minister can find a fruitful series of biographical studies here—possibly former pastors of the church, their
personalities and contributions to the growth and usefulness of the
church. Descendants of these men should be honored guests. Of
course, Bible characters are always a ready and valuable source for
setting forth God's manifestation of himself to men.

Whichever plan of preaching the minister is following, the midweek service should be creatively tied into it, whether parallel to or in contrast with what is done on Sunday. For instance, if the preaching program on Sundays calls for a series of sermons on men of God, the midweek service could give help through a series of messages on men of Satan. The Bible gives an abundance of both!

If the emphasis is upon world missions, beginning with city or associational missions and going "unto the uttermost parts of the earth," it is especially fitting and helpful to have a series of messages between Sunday services on missionaries, on institutions supported by missionary giving, on cities or countries where the denomination has missionary work, and the effectiveness or ineffectiveness of the denomination (and that particular church) in calling out young men and women for the missionary task.

Guidelines for the Service

Consider briefly some *guidelines of the midweek service*:

Prayer.—Whatever name the service may have, unless there is prayer—effective prayer—the service misses its purpose. Prayer is not the only purpose and guideline, but it is an indispensable one. The service should not give place to prayer, it should teach people how to pray. The need for this is obvious. The five-year-old son of a radio disc jockey in the San Francisco Bay area was heard to pray, "God bless Mommy, Daddy, Sister, amen and FM!"

The Bible.—At the center of the hour should be the Word of God. The message of the Bible should be delivered with variety and relevance. "A distinguished Catholic archaeologist who directed the excavation of the Dead Sea Scrolls said yesterday that the Bible must be the common building ground for the interfaith agreement," said the *San Francisco Chronicle* of Father DeVaux. The Bible is the ground not only for interfaith agreement, it is the ground for all faith agreement. It had best be kept at the center of the midweek hour.

Warmth.—The service should be characterized by spiritual warmth. There are many terms that might be used to characterize modern life; one that cannot be truthfully used is "spiritual warmth." Yet, without this quality, life can never be lived as God intended it to be lived. No Christian service can long be successful without due regard for this quality. Shortly before he died, novelist Eugene Burdick was asked if he should not take life more leisurely. The novelist answered: "No. I wouldn't want to settle for a longer life at a lower level." The midweek service must keep its temperature up.

Sharing.—The service should be one in which the people share. This can be done at many levels and in different ways. "Dialogue" is a word that has come into prominence; someone has said that it is a new word for the old word "argument." The midweek service does not need argument. It does need participation and sharing. Inhibitions need to be broken down. The people need to feel an "at-homeness."

Optimism.—There is too much of the note of failure in our public worship services. It is as if the administrators of the service believe that the devil has proved too much for God; that Christ has had his day; that the church has failed and the Bible is outdated. Where is the business enterprise that would not fail if it sounded such a note? Let the midweek service sound less of the flute and more of the trumpet!

Service.—The result of hearing the truth should be the doing of the truth. The author of 1 John accused those who walked in darkness of not "doing the truth." When a pompous lady asked Abraham Lincoln what his family coat of arms was, he answered: "My coat of arms is a pair of rolled-up sleeves." The midweek service should furnish inspiration, motive, and strength for doing church work, and for doing the work of the church—both are necessary, but the two are not the same.

Variety.—There are certain basic ingredients that need to be included in the midweek service—ingredients that *must* be included if the service is to be worthy. But there are different ways of mixing and blending these ingredients into the loaf of life. When a minister begins to give attention to variety, he may turn his between-Sunday service into an arena for an endless parade of novelties. "Pretty," "fresh," "new," "unusual," "exciting" gimmicks may be strung together in "an endless line of splendor" to take the place of carefully planned and solidly built services. Often the difficulty lies in the way an "idea" or an "approach" is used. As a single item in the overall service, used quickly and artistically to bring freshness and variety, to involve the people and to break down undesirable inhibitions, it would be good. Used to carry the main message and purpose of the service, it would be unworthy.

There is always some danger involved when a form is changed and a name is changed. Content may be changed, if done carefully. There is nothing particularly sacred about the form. More variety can be used in this service, and used in God-honoring ways, than in most other services.

Interest.—Variety will probably be needed to make the service interesting, but variety does not guarantee interest. If the service is not interesting, the service will not be effective. This requires careful planning. Sidney Smith is credited with saying that the sin against the Holy Ghost in the pulpit is dulness. It is the truth. There is nothing in this world or out of it, so far as anyone has discovered, that is as interesting, exciting, and dynamic as the grace of God revealed in the sacrificial love of Christ. To make that dull and uninteresting is a sin.

Numbers.—Numbers do not determine the value of a midweek service. In most school programs their effectiveness depends not upon an overrun classroom but on keeping the numbers small so that some individual attention can be given. It may be that one of the sources of potential strength for the midweek service is that there are fewer people to work with.

In 1848, Robert Lowe made a speech in the House of Commons and made light of "the battle of Marathon," because there were fewer people killed than are sometimes killed in a coal mine disaster. John Fisk responded that, using that guide, the newspaper was a better textbook than Herodotus. He felt that it was blindness to let the smallness in numbers keep one from seeing that the future of European civilization was tied up in the battle of Marathon. He said: "We cannot measure events with a foot rule."

But, it needs to be emphasized just as emphatically that small numbers do not guarantee power. A midweek service is not effective just because few people attend. The intent is to help people; it would be sinful for a service to help a hundred people only if it were possible for it to help two hundred people. It may well be that the proof of the effectiveness of our midweek services is not in numbers, but rather that our poor attendance is in some way tied up with the ineffectiveness of the services. Numbers are not the gauge; it is not by *few* or *many* that a man is helped.

Interlocking.—The midweek service needs to be tied to the rest of the plan for teaching and preaching, as noted above. It is not a place for solo work; it is a time for a symphony.

Relevance of the Service

As a rule, nothing takes the place of solid teaching and preaching for the major part of the midweek service. Following are suggestions that might be used to lend variety to the service.

There are ways of involving people in *prayer* at the midweek service.

1. Prayer can be personalized. Often the entire list of objects, persons, and causes are lumped together, and one person is asked to lead the prayer. It is helpful to spend a little time thinking about the person or object of prayer and then to assign some individual to pray for that particular object or person. When another object or person has been presented and lovingly thought about, call upon another person to pray for this person or object. When all the requests have been presented and thought about, the necessary and helpful facts given, and the person assigned to lead the prayer, the season of prayer can be engaged in with more concern and intelligence.

2. When the list of requests for prayer has been made, it can be understood that the pastor will call upon one individual to pray for one of the objects given. When this person has prayed, he may call the name of another person present who will pray personally for another object of prayer, and then on a third member of the group to continue the prayer by remembering another object or person. The prayers and the "tagging" can continue until all the objects have been taken to God in prayer.

3. The needs for prayer can be presented and the entire group divided into "prayer cells." These would go to different parts of the room, or to adjoining rooms for a season of prayer, each group taking as its concern one of the objects of prayer, the object having been assigned by the minister. The groups can be divided by rows, sections, or by numbers. The group may count off: 1, 2, 3, 4, 5, 6; 1, 2, 3, 4, 5, 6; until each person has a number. Those having "1" can go to the first group, those having "2" to the second group, and so on. A chairman for each cell would need to be appointed by the minister. A definite time limit will need to be announced.

4. If the atmosphere and the concern of the group is adequate, the pastor may ask for volunteers to come to the altar or the front of the room and kneel for a season of silent prayer while the organ or piano plays softly. When these have prayed for a brief season, they may return to their seats and others, without announcement, may take the places of those who have returned. This may continue until everyone who desires to do so has had an opportunity to come for prayer. It is well to prepare for this very carefully, perhaps by sharing your plan with a few individuals before the service. Suggest that if they feel led to do so, they come forward immediately when the opportunity is given. This will move the service along.

5. Volunteer "sentence" prayers are not very voluntary and they are usually much more than "sentence" prayers. A few individuals— the same individuals—pray, and they pray too long. We read that God will not hear a man for his "much speaking." So, careful guidance, early preparation, and prompting may be necessary if this form of prayer is to be helpful. It is valuable, and if sympathetically handled can be a blessing to many who will join their petition to those of their fellow worshipers. (It may be well to ask for a show of hands of those who will lead in sentence prayers.)

It is good for people to bear their *witness* before others in the warmth and helpfulness of a worship experience. The old "prayer meeting," or "testimony meeting," did this. It had its weaknesses, but, it did give the people a chance to be vocal about the deep things of faith. "They that feared the Lord spake often one to another: and the Lord hearkened, and heard it, and a book of remembrance was written before him for them that feared the Lord, and that thought upon his name" (Mal. 3:16).

For numerous reasons, this type of "testimony" meeting once known can be known no more. However, the best effects of such a meeting can still be experienced.

1. Hymns can be used as the basis for witnessing. Individuals can give their testimony in terms of these great hymns. What is your favorite hymn? Why? When and where and under what circumstances do you remember having heard it first?

2. When is your spiritual birthday? Where and under what conditions did you become a Christian? What type of service was it? Who was the pastor or preacher? Who was responsible for your making a decision at that time?

An added attraction for this idea is to have a large map and ask the people as they tell of this experience to come and mark the map at the spot, at least, the state, where they came to be numbered with the Lord's people.

3. Biographies are a means of grace. What life has meant the most to you? How old were you when you first read it? Who was responsible for leading you to read the book?

4. Who is your most unforgettable character and why? What did he do for you?

5. For what and for whom are you thankful? Tell us about it.

6. What is your most helpful and thrilling experience in the Christian life? Tell about it.

7. What is your favorite Bible verse? Why?

8. Have any of your prayers been answered? Tell us about it.

9. Have you read any good news this week: newspaper, book, magazine, TV, etc.? Tell us about it.

10. What do you remember about last Sunday's sermon? Was it helpful? Do you have questions about it? Do you have suggestions that you would like to make about the sermon if it is preached again?

The interview technique has been used to "get a story" in recent years. It offers many opportunities for the midweek service. There are many individuals who will consent to an interview who would not be willing to "make a speech." The interview can be controlled; questions can be asked that the people would like to have answered. Within a period of five minutes, more information can be secured from an interview than a twenty-minute address might yield. Think of a few individuals who might be profitably interviewed at the midweek service:

1. The oldest person in the church
2. The newest member of the church
3. A former pastor of the church
4. The pastor of a church of another denomination (Jewish rabbi, Catholic priest, Protestant minister)
5. Chief of the local police force: What are his problems? How can the church help?
6. A doctor
7. A nurse: suggestions about visiting the sick
8. A juvenile court judge
9. Superintendant of schools
10. Editor of the local paper
11. Local football coach
12. A beauty queen
13. A local mortician—funeral director
14. Interview a person about a missionary whose birthday comes on this particular day: where he serves; some of the problems he faces; some of his special needs.
15. Interview an individual who has made a careful study about some college, hospital, children's home, or other object to which the church contributes.
16. Interview a well-informed person about some country that is in the news, with special emphasis about the denomination's missionary program in that country.
17. Interview an author who has just had a book published or someone who has carefully read a new book on a theme that Christians need to know about.
18. Interview someone who has a serious handicap but has overcome it in a great way.

These suggestions can, of course, be multiplied. When the ideas are grouped together, there seems little that could put them into a well-planned program of preaching and teaching. Yet, this is just what planning does do. Whatever the overall theme for the week, month, season, or year may be, careful planning will make it possible to use such supporting material to give variety, interest, and added content.

Once more let it be said, the problem is not in the *use* of such ideas as suggested above but in their *misuse*. As supporting materials, as ways to involve the audience, as methods of securing interesting and valuable information, they are good. When they are used to carry the main weight and responsibility of the midweek service, they usually fail. Across the years a minister learns that nothing can be substituted for solid proclamation and careful teaching.

Variety in Preaching Forms

However, it is possible to preach the Word of God in different ways, and a new method of preaching may be used in the less formal midweek service when a minister would hesitate to use it at the more formal services on Sunday. After he has become familiar with the method and skilful in its use, and after the people who attend the midweek service have become familiar with it, the preacher may then use the method in the more formal atmosphere of the services held on Sunday.

A number of different forms of preaching are being tried, some of which seem to have had remarkable success. One of these is the use of *dialogue* in the pulpit. Every sensitive preacher seeks to involve his congregation in his sermon. Usually, there is no audible participation of the audience during the preaching, but the congregation may be mentally involved through the skilful use of question and answer, both on the part of the preacher. Or, the man in the pulpit may state fairly and honestly some position that he knows is held by persons in the audience, and then answer that question, objection, or criticism. Certain words, phrases, and asides can be used to carry on a one-sided dialogue with the audience.

There are certain direct ways, audible ways, of doing this also.

Some years ago such a project was carried out at historic Trinity Church in New York City. Trinity Church is in the heart of the financial (Wall Street) district—not a likely place for the gospel to get a hearing during the week. Yet thousands of people were attracted and stopped to listen to a method of preaching seldom heard since the Middle Ages. In the place of the "devil's advocate," there came into the pulpit an inquiring and bewildered layman. There he stood, toe to toe with the preacher, and raised biblical, doctrinal, and moral questions that were bothering him and, presumably, many in the audience. Then and there, the preacher dealt with the layman's difficulties in a constructive, sympathetic, biblical, and historical way.

The themes themselves are worthy of note, for it would seem that if hard, financially-minded, sophisticated New Yorkers could be persuaded to give these themes a hearing, then the method used would be worthy of consideration. The subjects used were "The End of the World," "Death and After Death," "Heaven and Hell," and "Kingdom Come."

Another form of the same general method of preaching was used at St. John's Cathedral, also in New York City. This series of sermons was preached in the evening. The sermons took the form of "trialogues" rather than dialogues. There were three persons in the pulpit. (These services were later broadcast over the A.B.C. radio network and received enthusiastic support.) Again, the layman was represented. He was the "middle man" and took the role of the tempted soul. On one side of the layman stood the "Tempter"; on the other side stood "The Voice," representing the Spirit. There, in the pulpit, before the eyes of the congregation, the struggle for the soul of man took place. The trialogues dealt with the classic seven deadly sins: wrath, lust, envy, gluttony, covetousness, sloth, pride, and original sin.

The biographical sermon is not new; it is one of the ancient and ever-popular homiletic forms. But the imaginative narrative, or autobiographical monologue-impersonation, is being used more and more widely. Here the sermon is told in first person rather than in third. Instead of the preacher bringing a sermon on the life and message of the prophet Hosea, the preacher assumes the role of Hosea and lets the prophet tell his own story. Or, instead of hearing a sermon on Peter's denials, the audience hears Peter tell his own story of the denials. Sometimes this is done in costume.

Some years ago the minister in one of the great pulpits of America did a series of such sermons on the prophets. He was carefully costumed for the different prophets. He bears witness that in all his years of preaching he never communicated with his audience more effectively.

Another potentially helpful approach is to have the preacher and an assistant or assistants assume the role of different Bible characters. The churches have always been interested in and disturbed about the incident that tells of Peter, Ananias, and Sapphira as recorded in the fifth chapter of Acts. Let these three individuals explain, defend, apologize for themselves. Or, let Paul and Barnabas declare the wonderful works of God that took place during the infancy of the Christian movement.

These are a few different ways of proclaiming the gospel that may be used in the midweek services. A few cautions are in order: Never confuse the method with the message; the gospel must be proclaimed. No form that is worthy is easy; these forms, like all others, call for careful preparation and hard work. They are not for the lazy man. If the preacher is a relative of the sorry character in the Scriptures who complained, "I cannot do it," he might as well forget these forms. But, then, such a man should not be in the ministry anyway, should he?

13
Planning
Scripture Readings

There was a time when people came to the churches to hear the Bible read. The churches were the only places the people could hear the Bible read, for the churches were the only places the Bible could be found, and the priests were the only persons who could read. The Bibles were chained to the pulpits. The people came; the priests read. Everywhere else the Bible was a closed book.

That was a long time ago and conditions have changed. Today Bibles can be purchased in department stores, drugstores, grocery stores, and chain stores, as well as in book stores. The prices are within range of nearly everyone. The people can read. But, they do not read—not the Bible! This is true not just for the "unchurched"; it is also true for the average church member. It is legitimate to raise the question, Is the person who will not read the Bible any better off than the person who cannot read the Bible? In a very real sense, conditions are similar today to conditions that existed hundreds of years ago. About the only place modern-day man hears the Bible read is in the churches at a service of public worship.

This makes clear the necessity for including the place of the Scriptures as a part of a planned preaching program. Dr. Luther A. Weigle, formerly dean of the Yale Divinity School, said that no matter what other duties the minister had, "unless the Word of God be rightly and effectively read and preached and taught, no ministry meets the people's need as it should." The public reading of the Bible is not an "elective" in public worship; it is a "required" course. It is not for the purpose of giving a springboard for the sermon; it has a ministry all its own.

Why the Bible Has to Be Read

Some time ago, Arlan Dohrenburg wrote of a sharp young lady of sixteen confronting him with, "Why do ministers *have* to read the Bible out loud in church? I guess I shouldn't say this, but I'd much rather we just had five minutes of absolute silence so a person could quietly read the lesson for himself."

The young lady's question deserves an answer. *Why do ministers have to read the Bible in the service of public worship?* To begin, they are directed to do so. The direction comes from God. There were laws laid down for reading the Word of God in the synagogues. Preaching was optional, but reading the Scriptures was required! In the eighth chapter of Nehemiah it is recorded: "So they read in the book in the law of God distinctly, and gave the sense, and caused them to understand the reading" (v. 8). And Timothy received the instruction, "Till I come, attend to the public reading of the Scriptures, to preaching, to teaching" (1 Tim. 4:13, RSV).

The reading of the Bible in services of public worship perpetuates a custom and a means of worship that was taken over by the early churches from the ancient synagogue. When Jesus went into the synagogue at Nazareth on the sabbath, they gave him the scroll of Isaiah and he read from it. Few things that we do in our services of worship have so long and honored a tradition as the public reading of the Scriptures. At first the early churches read the Law and the Prophets; later they read the Gospels and the Epistles. The Bible has been "appointed to be read in the churches."

In the second place, the Bible has to be read in the churches because of what Paul wrote to Timothy: "All scripture . . . is profitable for doctrine, for reproof, for correction, for instruction in righteousness" (2 Tim. 3:16). The point of that quotation is that the Scriptures throw the light of God's evaluation upon life and everything that man does. It is as the sun going forth from the ends of the heavens. There is nothing hid from it—no need, no sin, no grief, no joy, no tragedy, no victory. John Hutton once said that the Bible was a strong searchlight by which a man could read the fine print of his own soul.

W. A. Visser't Hooft wrote of his people: "In Holland, the people thought that the Bible must contain dynamite since the Nazis were so anxious to destroy it. So they reopened its pages to find the dynamite—and they found it." [1] That has been the experience of the oppressed and harassed through the centuries. The little girl declared to her friend: "I tell you, the Bible does not end in Timothy; it ends in Revolutions." When Shaphan the scribe read the Law to the king and the king called the nation together and caused the Law to be read to them, there was a great reformation. The Bible proved itself to be "profitable for doctrine, for reproof, for correction, for instruction in righteousness."

There is a third reason for reading the Bible in the public service of worship: it positions the minister. In the main, Protestants have kept the pulpit in the center of their places of worship; upon the pulpit they have kept the open Bible; behind the open Bible they have placed their minister. The whole arrangement is a powerful symbol—more than a symbol, but a powerful symbol. It has said to all who have come within the church's gates: "We are a people who believe in the Word of God. We believe in the spoken Word because it is based upon the written Word; and we believe in the written Word because it reveals the living Word."

This chosen representative of ours who speaks to us of the living Word, does not speak on his own authority. He comes to us on the authority of the living Word as revealed in—not completely in, but never contrary to—the written Word.

A fourth reason for reading the Bible in public worship is that the Word of God can best be understood when it is read aloud. It is possible to say, and truthfully, that the Bible cannot be read effectively until it is understood; but it is equally true, from another valid point of view, that the Bible cannot be understood until it is read aloud. Much of the Bible was written for this definite purpose, written in private to be read in public—"ordained to be read in the churches." And it was written in private to be read in public to ordinary people for their instruction, for their guidance and help.

There is a sense in which many great pieces of literature come alive only as they are read aloud to an appreciative audience. This is true whether it be Shakespeare, Browning, Dickens, or Frost. But, the public reading of the Bible is more than this. When God's people listen attentively to his Word, a mystical presence joins the company. Whether the group is large or small, two or three, or two or three thousand, he is in the midst.

Why the Bible Is Read Poorly

These, then, are some of the reasons why the Bible is read in public worship. The young lady who first asked the question wanted to know why the minister always had to read the Bible; she preferred a period of silence in which the individual would be allowed to read the Bible for himself. Dr. Dohrenburg asked why. The young lady continued: "Because the ministers I hear put so little into it—or get so little out of it. I don't know which—maybe both. When I read it myself, I get all sorts of feelings. When they read it, I usually just feel bored."

So! Actually, the problem is not that the Bible is read, but that it is read poorly. The young lady should not be dealt with too harshly. She is only saying what many a worshiper feels. *One of the most uninteresting parts of the average Sunday morning service of worship is the time when the Bible is read aloud by the minister.* Why?

First, the minister often does not believe that it is important for him to read well. There are few men who could not read effectively if they were willing to pay the price required in time, discipline, and dedication. Since they do not do this, it must be assumed that they do not believe it is sufficiently important.

Second, the Bible is read poorly because the minister has a superficial familiarity with it; this superficial familiarity leads him to assume that no further effort is required on his part. He has heard the passage read many times; he has read it many times himself; he has studied the passage (maybe) during the week as he prepared his sermon. He can pronounce every word in the passage. And so, he assumes that he is prepared to read the passage in public worship.

But a special type of preparation is required for an effective, interpretive reading of the Bible. It is not enough to be able to pronounce the words, even to understand the meaning of the words. This is necessary, but is is not enough. Some years ago when a learned book came off the press, a friend asked a colleague of the author if he had read the book. The colleague answered: "Yes, I have read it."

"Did you understand it?"

"I understood every word—but not a single sentence."

There is a third reason the Bible is read poorly. The minister thinks it is easy to read the Bible. If he can pronounce the words, get through without too much stumbling, and make himself reasonably well heard, this is the full requirement. Someone needs to say to such a minister: "If you mouthe it, as many readers do, I would as live the town crier read the verses. Be not too tame either; but let your own discretion be your tutor. Suit the volume to the meaning and the meaning to the volume. O the readers I have heard read!" [2] The honest fact is this, it is exceedingly difficult to read the Bible effectively.

There is a fourth reason for poor reading. The attention of the reader is divided. He is thinking of that part of the service that has gone before, of that part of the service that is to come after; he is thinking that the room is too warm or too cold; the windows need to be opened, closed, or the thermostat needs to be turned up or down. Will the ushers be alert and realize that only three verses, not four, of the offertory hymn are being sung? Will that mother, bless her, take that fretful and disturbing child to the nursery, or shall I have to compete? Why does the organist keep the volume down when we sing this new hymn? Now, why are the Smiths absent today? Did he resent that remark made in the meeting of the Finance Committee? I cannot see that Murray boy in the audience; I had hoped he would be here today and make his decision for Christ. Wow! Look at that hat! Now, what is the third line in that quatrain I wanted to quote this morning?

So, the attention is divided. The Scripture lesson is to be read; the passage is marked. As long as that bird is in the hand, the attention of the minister flits to every bush and tree of interest. No man can read the Scriptures worthily unless that task has his undivided attention.

It is like taking a young lady out to dinner and giving your attention to everyone and everything except the young lady. She sees you bowing and turning and smiling to everyone in the room. She knows that you are preoccupied, that although she has your full poundage in the seat beside her, she most certainly does not have your undivided attention. That little flirt at the next table has too much of it. And through her smiles and witty remarks, she is saying, "This is a wretched evening; just wait 'til he asks me for another date!"

Look at another reason for poor reading. The minister may consciously or unconsciously imitate another. In the past he has heard someone whom he greatly admired read aloud. As this person read, certain things stood out about his reading: accents, emphasis, timing, volume, and rate. It is so easy to copy these. It is not often realized that when one imitates another, it is usually the most undesirable qualities of that person's performance that are copied. Nor is it realized that the person being copied is effective in spite of these eccentricities.

How to Read Helpfully

The Bible can be effectively read in the service of public worship. This would be possible, it may be said, by reversing what have been given as the major reasons for ineffective reading of the Bible. But guidelines for effective reading need to be spelled out fully.

The minister will have to believe that the public reading of the Scriptures is important—indeed, that this reading may well be *the most important part* of the service. He will need to remember that in the past God has used the public reading of the Scriptures as a means of speaking to his people, and that if God does not seem to do so today, the minister has to assume a part of the responsibility.

Preaching is an "I-You" relationship—man speaking to man.

Praying takes on the relationship of "I-Thou"—sinful man speaking to holy God. Public reading of the Word of God is a "Thou-I" relationship—holy God speaking to sinful man.

These relationships are not being placed in airtight, theologically tight, compartments. There is mutual sharing and visiting back and forth across the lines of the relationships. Still, the different areas may logically and doctrinally be so defined. When these areas are so seen, who would be so bold as to say that the public reading of the Word of God is any less important than preaching or prayer? Surely, what God says to man is as important as what man says to man, even though it be on the authority of God, and as important as what man says to God, even though man be prompted and taught by the Spirit of God. The words of Samuel are as valid and as needed today as when they were first uttered: "Speak, Lord; for thy servant heareth." John L. Casteel has said,

When the Word is read, we know how God, "Who at sundry times and in divers manners spake in time past unto the fathers by the prophets, hath in these last days spoken to us by his Son," even unto us in the living, present moment. We feel ourselves to be one with the great movement which His Word initiates and sustains in history; we are edified and instructed in righteousness; and we are drawn into communion with those who hear, with us, His Word through faith, and with Him who speaks. To read and to hear the Word with the congregation is to enter into one of the deepest moments of worship.[3]

The minister's attitude toward the public reading of the Bible will be communicated to the people. His attitude will show that he thinks the place of the public reading of the Word of God should either be put under a bushel or on a lampstand, for there is no real attitude toward this part of the service that shall not be revealed, and no hidden part that shall not be known.

A Valid Part of the Service

In the second place, if the Bible is to be read helpfully, the minister must consider it an integral and valid part of the service in its own right and not just as an appendage, springboard, or tag for his sermon. Often the reading—the amount, placing, and use of it—suggests that its only purpose is homiletical. The Scriptures are made subservient to the sermon; their only purpose in the service is to "legitimatize" the sermon. This is a debasement of the Word of God!

A proper understanding of the Bible, of our Protestant comprehension of it, gives ample place for both the read Word and the preached Word. God will speak through both if each is given its due in attention and preparation. Seldom are we justified in neglecting either in a regular service of public worship.

It should never be forgotten that from the standpoint of biblical history, church history, practical effectiveness, and sheer fair play, the public reading of the Word of God has a legitimate ticket of its own to ride on the eleven o'clock train, or any other hour's train of public worship. The Bible has this "ticket" on at least two counts: from the standpoint of devotion and the standpoint of education. These two grounds are not distinct; they are never mutually exclusive of each other.

The typical Minister's Conference will usually have some variety. But, there is one lecture and emphasis that is seldom absent; it returns again and again like the proverbial old refrain. It is the lament over the departed expository sermon. The absence of this type of preaching is credited with being responsible for many ills that plague humans, from a dropping off in the number of baptisms and the true nurture of the saints to the mounting divorce rate and the skyrocketing of the crime wave. The charge might be answered in different ways; there might be some agreement and some disagreement, some questions and some soul searching.

It is strange, however, that there should be such universal agreement as to the need for expository preaching, and yet such neglect of the vehicle for its use. Unquestionably, the most effective exposition of the Scriptures open to the average minister is competent interpretative reading of them. Besides, while effective expository preaching is "high and lifted up," so much so that few men can do it well, almost any minister could (if he would) do effective expository reading.

If the Bible is to be read effectively in the service of worship, there is a third thing that the minister needs to do. He must carefully plan where he will place the reading in the overall order of service. Radio and television people know the value of this. The placing of a program or a spot announcement is enhanced or penalized by the place it is given in the total program, by what goes before and by what comes after, and by the way the announcement is introduced. Management, certainly those who pay for the "spot," would not want the promotion of a retirement home for senior citizens to come immediately before an advertisement for a funeral home or a local cemetery.

One of the accepted and worthy movements of a worship service that is often used, with addition for enrichment or subtraction for simplification, is as follows:

Preparation:	Organ meditation
Recognition:	Call to worship, invocation, response
Aspiration:	Responsive reading (if used), hymn
Communication:	Scripture reading, silence, prayer, response
Dedication:	Offertory hymn, sentence, offering, anthem, doxology, prayer, response
Illumination:	Sermon
Commitment:	Invitation, hymn
Embarkation:	Benediction, response, silence, organ postlude

Such an order of service places the Scripture lesson where it will be given due theological and psychological emphasis. The people will have been brought into a spirit where God can speak to mind and heart through his Word.

In the fourth place, if the public reading of the Bible is to make the contribution that its purpose justifies, the lessons must be chosen with great care. If any minister will list the Scripture passages that he has read to his people during the past twelve months, he will immediately see how much he needs help.

William F. Dunkel, Jr. has said that there is one part of the judicial oath that ministers fail to live up to in their Scripture readings. The oath requires that a witness "tell the truth, the whole truth, and nothing but the truth." Dunkel says that the minister lives up to the first and last part of the oath rather well; it is at the point of telling the *whole* truth that he falls down.[4] The average minister reads precious little (what he reads is precious and there is little of it!) of the total Word of God.

Yet, there are few ministers who would say that the great blocks of Scripture that he neglects are not a part of the Word of God; if quizzed, he would agree that those sections that he seldom, if ever, reads do have value. Yet, practically, he never lets God speak to his people in the use of these blocks of Scripture. It is not a comfortable thought to the "free" churchman to realize that the more "liturgical" ministers have done a better job at giving their people the advantage of the whole Word of God. Yet, an honest evaluation would lead to that conclusion.

The reason for this is a simple one: the liturgical churches have used lectionaries.

Using the Lectionary

There is much to be said for such a practice. The selections of Scripture made by a good lectionary are of reasonable length and wisely chosen. The use of a lectionary follows an emphasis upon the Christian Year, thereby giving a worthy accent upon great events in the life of Christ and the people of God. Over a period of a year, or years, the people are introduced to the main sections of the entire Bible, rather than being subjected to a tedious repetition of a few choice bits of Scripture.

Generally speaking, if a minister uses a standard lectionary as guide, he will read selected passages from the gospels and Epistles, possibly a Psalm, on the days when the Lord's Supper is observed. On other Sundays he will read a Psalm, an Old Testament lesson, and a New Testament lesson. In liturgical terms the Psalms are not considered a part of the Old Testament lesson nor a substitute for it; Acts and Revelation are placed with the Epistles.

Where will lectionaries be found? Most of the minister's annuals include them. The books on worship published by numerous denominations carry them. If a minister is willing to pay the price, he may make his own lectionary, in which case the standard ones give valuable guidance. The idea of the planned Scripture lessons is similar to that followed by the International Sunday School lesson plans for many years. In order to assure a coverage of the whole Bible, a five-year cycle of lessons are agreed upon.

The wise use of the lectionaries have attempted to make it possible for the ministers and churches to "declare the whole counsel of God."

It means exactly that [says Robbins]. It means teaching the whole of the truth that Christ revealed; all the virtues he enjoined; all the means of grace which he employed; all the hope of glory which he opened; the whole bearing of his gospel upon thought, speech and behaviour. How can this or anything resembling it be done without a plan. Every successful teacher knows the answer to such a question and prepares his course of instruction accordingly.[5]

Go a step further. If the public reading of the Bible is to be really helpful, the minister must make careful preparation for the reading. This note was sounded earlier when it was affirmed that one of the reasons for failure is that proper preparation is not made. The late and greatly beloved Peter Marshall wrote:

I have a feeling that no part of the average Protestant service needs more attention and receives less than the reading of the Scriptures. Let the minister remember that he is reading the Word of God, and not the curb market quotations from yesterday's newspaper. Let him practice reading the chosen selection, until he is sure that he can reveal its meaning in his inflection. If the meaning is not clear to him, he will never be able to make it clear to his congregation . . . the minister must feel what he reads, and not stumble through it as if he were seeing it for the first time, and had not the slightest idea as to what it might mean. This is one part of the service where God is speaking to the people through his Word, and the voice of the minister. Nothing should be allowed to interrupt or detract from this part of the service. Quiet and revered attention is more becoming at this part of the service than at any other, for here God is speaking to us . . . there is absolutely no excuse for slipshod, unintelligent reading of the Holy Scriptures. No greater mistake could be made than to assume that it is easy to read the

Bible. It is one of the most difficult parts of the service, and one which the sensible preacher will approach with preparation and dedication.[6]

The minister's preparation for reading the particular Scripture lessons should include such items as the following: attention to the particular type of Scripture—Law, prophecy, history, poetry, Gospel, Epistle. Who was the author? What type of individual was he? What were his mood and spirit as he wrote the passage? What was he trying to say to those to whom he spoke or wrote? How can the author's intent and purpose best be interpreted?

Remember, as a reader the minister is an interpreter; he is expounding what God's Spirit led the writer to say. Careful attention must be given to the actual reading. The minister must remember that the word which God is seeking to speak to the people, God is seeking to say to the minister, also. It was said of old minister Struthers of Greenock, Scotland, that he never seemed to be reading the Scriptures as if he had written them, but always as if he were listening to a voice!

Finally, there is more value in a great and beautiful pulpit Bible than merely the size of the print that makes it easy for the minister to read. There is significant symbolism in a center pulpit with a Bible on it, and a man of God behind both, proclaiming God. There is something impressive about the very size and position of the Book. Instead of a small Testament or Bible that the minister takes from his pocket—one that is stuffed with envelopes, Sunday School materials, and notes on the sick—here is an impressive and imposing book, beautifully bound, free of papers and notes, opened at the first lesson with the second lesson marked. Let it always be handled with respect.

In spite of its known imperfections, the King James Version is best for pulpit use. This is not to say that other translations and versions will not be read from the pulpit. It is to say that the minister will want to read from the King James more often than he will from any other; there are certain passages that he will hesitate to read from any but the King James—the twenty-third Psalm, Isaiah 53, John 3:16, and John 14 are among these. Therefore, it is best for the pulpit Bible to be in the King James Version; the minister can then bring other translations to the pulpit as they are needed.

What About Congregational Reading?

In certain parts of the country, and among some groups in those sections, the custom of having persons in the congregation bring their Bibles to the worship hour, turn to the chosen Scripture lesson and read along silently with the minister when the lesson is being read, is emphasized. If the purpose of the public reading of the Bible is to hear what God would say to his people when they are met together as the body of Christ, it is doubtful that the practice of joint reading is helpful.

In an average congregation there are many different translations. Although the message is the same, the words are different. People do not read with equal speed. Some rush ahead of the minister, some lag behind, and some will pause to question a word. There is delay and often disturbance in finding places in the Bibles. If the minister has prepared in mind and in heart for careful interpretive reading, if the people will listen carefully and prayerfully, it is almost certain that they will more nearly get the meaning and the intent of God than if they follow word for word, line for line in their own Bibles Of course, if there is some mystical value in the handling of a Bible itself, in looking at the words, in mentally pronouncing individual words, then the custom may be a worthy one.

Much of the same point can be made about responsive readings. This is a custom that comes and goes. A little over twenty-five years ago, the responsive reading was being emphasized in the seminaries, in books and magazines, in conferences and pastor's schools. There followed a period when little was written about it and less was done about its practice. Now, there are indications in some quarters that the responsive reading may be on the upswing again. Religious educators are emphasizing the importance of bringing small children to the services of worship; it is urged, and surely the point is well taken, that when the child is present in the service, he should be made to feel a part of the service by participating in all of its parts.

It is difficult for the average church to have a worship experience through a responsive reading. It is easy to see some of the problems. Observe the next service you attend where the responsive reading is used. Again, all adults do not read with the same speed. Some lag behind, some rush ahead, some stumble over words, some begin reading too early, some are reading aloud when others have stopped. This causes embarrassment. Often the selections used for responsive readings are not well chosen and helpfully arranged. So, the value of the responsive reading of the Scriptures would seem to be questionable. One thing is sure: *The responsive reading should not take the place of the careful reading of the Word of God by the minister.*

Come back to the question, "Why do ministers read the Bible so poorly in church?" The answer to that is, the minister does not have to read the Bible poorly in church. He can so read it that it will be a rich and meaningful experience for him and for his people.

In Nehemiah 8:5-8 the record says: "Ezra opened the book in the sight of all the people; (for he was above all the people;) . . . and Ezra blessed the Lord, the great God. And all the people answered, Amen, Amen, . . . and they bowed their heads, and worshipped the Lord with their faces to the ground. . . . So they read in the book in the law of God distinctly, and gave the sense, and caused them to understand the reading." Perhaps something like this may be the experience of the modern-day congregation as the minister makes the public reading of the Bible a part of his preaching plan.

Or, perhaps the minister can provide for his people—through a planned preaching program which includes carefully planned Scripture reading—something like that experienced by those who attended the synagogue when Jesus read. It was in Nazareth; the attendant brought the Scriptures to Jesus. Jesus stood to read, "and the eyes of all [the people] . . . were fastened on him. . . . And all bare him witness, and wondered at the gracious words which proceeded out of his mouth" (Luke 4:20-22).

Notes

Chapter 1

1. G. K. Chesterton, *The Autobiography of G. K. Chesterton* (London and New York: Sheed & Ward, 1954), p. 218.
2. Charles M. Crow, *The Best of the Sanctuary* (New York: Abingdon Press, 1963), p. 26.
3. Only three major denominations will be considered in listing the events: Southern Baptist, Methodist, and United Presbyterian. Events pertaining only to Baptists will be checked with a "B"; Methodists, with an "M"; and Presbyterians, with a "P." Events observed by each will not be starred. Of course, some of the events will vary in time as much as a month, so the dates would always need to be checked carefully.

Chapter 2

1. Quoted by J. S. Stewart, *Heralds of God* (New York: Charles Scribner's Sons, 1946), p. 173.
2. Sylva Porter, *San Francisco Chronicle,* June 25, 1965, p. 56.
3. Halford E. Luccock, *The Minister's Workshop* (New York: Abingdon Press, 1954), p. 202.
4. *San Francisco Chronicle,* January 10, 1965, p. 24.

Chapter 3

1. Quoted in Victor E. Beck and Paul M. Lindberg, *A Book of Advent* (Philadelphia: Fortress Press, 1963) p. 68.

Chapter 4

1. From *Worship Resources for the Christian Year,* ed. by Charles L. Wallis. By permission of Harper & Row, Publishers. See page 9.
2. Donald G. Miller, *Fire in Thy Mouth* (New York: Abingdon Press, 1954), p. 17.
3. Approach suggested by Evelyn Underhill, *Worship* (New York: Harper & Bros., 1937), pp. 74–77.

Chapter 5

1. Based on outline in C. H. Dodd, *The Apostolic Preaching* (Chicago: Willett, Clark & Co., 1937), pp. 25–29.
2. J. S. Stewart, *Heralds of God* (New York: Charles Scribner's Sons, 1946), p. 111.
3. Horton Davies, *Varieties of English Preaching, 1900–1960* (Englewood Cliffs, N. J.: Prentice-Hall, 1963), p. 215.
4. Hugh C. Warner, *Daily Readings from William Temple* (Nashville: Abingdon Press, 1950), pp. 271–72.
5. Leonard Griffith, *God's Time and Ours* (Nashville: Abingdon Press, 1964), p. 29.
6. Karl Rahner, *The Eternal Year* (Baltimore: Helicon Press, 1964), p. 21.
7. See my *Seven First Words of Jesus* (Nashville: Broadman Press, 1966), pp. 82 ff.
8. From *Worship Resources for the Christian Year*, ed. by Charles L. Wallis. By permission of Harper & Row, Publishers. See page 43.
9. *Ibid.*, p. 87.

Chapter 6

1. Gerald Kennedy, "The Starting Line," *Pulpit Digest*, XLVI (October, 1965), 57–58.
2. Herschel H. Hobbs in a personal letter to the author.
3. As quoted in John Baillie, *A Diary of Readings* (New York: Charles Scribner's Sons, 1955), p. 187.
4. Edna St. Vincent Millay, *Conversation at Midnight* (New York: Harper & Bros., 1937), p. 30.
5. Quoted in J. Wallace Hamilton, *The Thunder of Bare Feet* (Westwood, N. J.: Fleming H. Revell Co., 1964), p. 147.
6. Halford E. Luccock, *Communicating the Gospel* (New York: Harper & Bros., 1954), pp. 103–4.

Chapter 7

1. Harry Emerson Fosdick, "What Is the Matter with Preaching?" *Harper's Magazine* (July, 1928).
2. Quoted in Robert E. Luccock, *Halford Luccock Treasury* (Nashville: Abingdon Press, 1963), p. 156.
3. Fosdick, *The Living of These Days* (New York: Harper & Bros., 1956), p. 95.
4. Quoted in Morgan Phelps Noyes, *Preaching the Word of God* (New York: Charles Scribner's Sons, 1943), pp. 126–27.
5. Quoted in A. J. William Myers, *Enriching Worship* (New York: Harper & Bros., 1949), p. 36.
6. Gabriel J. Fackre, *The Pastor and the World* (Philadelphia: United Church Press, 1964), p. 42.

7. *Ibid.*, p. 45.

8. John W. Doberstein, *Minister's Prayer Book* (Philadelphia: Muhlenberg (Fortress) Press, 1959), p. 250.

9. Joseph R. Sizoo, *Preaching Unashamed* (New York: Abingdon Press, 1959), p. 23.

10. Thornton Wilder, *Skin of Our Teeth* in *Three Plays* (New York: Harper & Bros., 1957).

Chapter 8

1. Herb Caen, *San Francisco Chronicle,* January 10, 1965.

Chapter 9

1. *Southern Baptist Convention Annual,* 1965 (Nashville: Executive Committee, 1965), p. 267.

2. Hugh C. Warner, *Daily Readings from William Temple* (Nashville: Abingdon Press, 1950), p. 51.

3. Herb Caen, *San Francisco Chronicle,* January 3, 1966, p. 25.

Chapter 10

1. Bryan Green, *The Practice of Evangelism* (New York: Charles Scribner's Sons, 1951), p. 6.

2. Gabriel J. Fackre, *The Pastor and the World* (Philadelphia: United Church Press, 1964), p. 192.

3. Jacob Trapp, *Modern Religious Poems* (New York: Harper & Row, 1964), p. 192.

4. "The Appalling Erosions of Moral Standards," *San Francisco Examiner,* February 27, 1966, Sec. 2, p. 2.

5. Peter Abrahams, *Tell Freedom* (New York: Alfred A. Knopf, 1954).

6. Green, *op. cit.,* pp. 84–5.

7. A. J. Lerner and F. Loewe, *Camelot* (New York: Random House, 1961).

8. *San Francisco Chronicle,* January 18, 1966, p. 39.

9. Pierce Harris, "Keep It Simple, Preacher, or Your Sanctuary Suffers," *Atlanta Journal* (Georgia), January 19, 1966.

Chapter 11

1. J. S. Whale, *Christian Doctrine* (New York: The Macmillan Co., 1941), p. 157.

2. Emil Brunner, *Our Faith* (London: SCM Press, 1936), p. 127.

3. Harold E. Fey, *The Lord's Supper: Seven Meanings* (New York: Harper & Bros., 1948), p. 8.

4. Quoted by Halford E. Luccock, "Daily Meditations," *Christian Herald,* LXXX, No. 4 (April, 1957), 40.

5. Hugh Thompson Kerr, *The Christian Sacraments* (Philadelphia: The Westminster Press, 1954), p. 28.

6. Quoted in Robert E. Luccock, *Halford Luccock Treasury* (Nashville: Abingdon Press, 1963), p. 401.

Chapter 13

1. Charles L. Wallis (ed.), *A Treasury of Sermon Illustrations* (Nashville: Abingdon Press, 1950), p. 27.
2. William Shakespeare, *Hamlet*.
3. John L. Casteel, *Religion in Life* (Spring, 1944), p. 240.
4. William Frederick Dunkle, Jr., *Values in the Church Year* (Nashville: Abingdon Press, 1959), p. 89.
5. Howard Robbins, *Preaching the Gospel* (New York: Harper & Bros., 1939), p. 12.
6. Peter Marshall, *Religion in Life* (Spring, 1945), p. 203.

Selected Readings

Planning Your Preaching

Abbey, Merrill R. *Living Doctrine in a Vital Pulpit*. New York: Abingdon Press, 1964.

Blackwood, Andrew W. *Plannning a Year's Pulpit Work*. Nashville: Abingdon Press, 1952.

————. *Doctrinal Preaching for Today*. New York: Abingdon Press, 1956.

Gibson, George Miles. *Planned Preaching*. Philadelphia: The Westminster Press, 1954.

Jones, Ilion T. *Principles and Practice of Preaching*. New York: Abingdon Press, 1956.

MacLennan, David A. *Resources for Sermon Preparation*. Philadelphia: The Westminster Press, 1957.

Macleod, Donald. *Here Is My Method*. Westwood, N. J.: Fleming H. Revell Co., 1952.

Whitesell, F. D., and Perry, L. M. *Variety in Your Preaching*. Westwood, N. J.: Fleming H. Revell Co., 1954.

Stidger, William L. *Planning Your Preaching*. New York: Harper & Bros., 1932.

Brown, H. C., Jr. *Southern Baptist Preaching*. Nashville: Broadman Press, 1959.

————. *More Southern Baptist Preaching*. Nashville: Broadman Press, 1964.

The Christian Year

Blackwood, Andrew W. *This Year of Our Lord*. Philadelphia: The Westminster Press, 1953.

Dunkle, William F., Jr. *Values in the Church Year*. New York: Abingdon Press, 1959.

Forell, George W. *The Christian Year*. New York: Thomas Nelson & Sons, 1964.

Gibson, George M. *The Story of the Christian Year*. New York: Abingdon Press, 1955.

Griffith, Leonard. *God's Time and Ours*. New York: Abingdon Press, 1964.

Holcraft, Paul E. *Texts and Themes for the Christian Year*. New York: Abingdon Press, 1957.

Hardin, H. G., *et al*. *The Celebration of the Gospel*. New York: Abingdon Press, 1964.

Hauck, Allen. *Calendar of Christianity*. New York: Association Press, 1961.

Johnson, Howard A. *Preaching the Christian Year*. New York: Charles Scribner's Sons, 1957.

MacLennan, David A. *Preaching Week By Week*. Westwood, N. J.: Fleming H. Revell Co., 1963.

Wallis, Charles L. *Worship Resources for the Christian Year*. New York: Harper & Bros., 1954.

————. *Lenten-Easter Sourcebook*. New York: Abingdon Press, 1961.

Weiser, Francis X. *Handbook of Christian Feasts and Customs*. New York: Harcourt, Brace & World, 1958.

Preaching Through the Bible

Anderson, Bernard W. *Rediscovering the Bible*. New York: Association Press, 1951.

Blackwood, Andrew W. *Preaching from the Bible*. Nashville: Abingdon Press, 1951.

————. *Expository Preaching for Today*. New York: Abingdon Press, 1953.

————. *Biographical Preaching for Today*. New York: Abingdon Press, 1954.

Coffin, Henry Sloane. *What to Preach*. Peterborough, N. H.: The Richard R. Smith Co., 1930.

Farmer, Herbert H. *The Servant of the Word*. New York: Charles Scribner's Sons, 1942.

Faw, Chalmer E. *A Guide to Biblical Preaching*. Nashville: Broadman Press, 1962.

Ford, D. W. Cleverley. *An Expository Preacher's Notebook*. New York: Harper & Bros., 1960.

Kennedy, Gerald. *His Word Through Preaching*. New York: Harper & Bros., 1947.

Miller, Donald G. *The Way to Biblical Preaching*. New York: Abingdon Press, 1957.

Neill, William. *The Rediscovery of the Bible*. New York: Harper & Bros., 1954.

Pearce, J. Winston. *Paul and His Letters*. Nashville: Broadman Press, 1961.

Roach, Corwin C. *Preaching Values in the Bible*. Louisville: Cloister Press, 1946.

Pearson, Roy. *The Preacher: His Purpose and Practice*. Philadelphia: The Westminster Press, 1962.

Richardson, Alan. *A Preface to Bible Study.* Philadelphia: The Westminster Press, 1944.

Stevenson, Dwight E. *Preaching on the Books of the New Testament.* New York: Harper & Bros., 1956.

―――. *Preaching on the Books of the Old Testament.* New York: Harper & Row, 1961.

Swaim, J. Carter. *Right and Wrong Ways to Use the Bible.* Philadelphia: The Westminster Press, 1953.

Thomas, George Brown. *What Shall I Preach.* Nashville: Abingdon Press, 1948.

Preaching to Meet People's Needs

Cleland, James T. *Preaching to Be Understood.* New York: Abingdon Press, 1965.

Coffin, Henry Sloane. *Communion Through Preaching.* New York: Charles Scribner's Sons, 1952.

Edwards, Richard Henry. *A Person-Minded Ministry.* Nashville: Abingdon Press, 1940.

Ferris, Theodore Parker. *Go Tell the People.* New York: Charles Scribner's Sons, 1951.

Garrison, Webb B. *Creative Imagination in Preaching.* New York: Abingdon Press, 1960.

Luccock, Halford E. *In the Minister's Workshop.* New York: Abingdon Press, 1954.

―――. *Communicating the Gospel.* New York: Harper & Bros., 1954.

MacLennan, David A. *Pastoral Preaching.* Philadelphia: The Westminster Press, 1955.

Jackson, Edgar N. *How to Preach to People's Needs.* New York: Abingdon Press, 1956.

―――. *A Psychology for Preaching.* New York: Abingdon Press, 1961.

Sellers, James E. *The Outsider and the Word of God.* New York: Abingdon Press, 1961.

Teikmanis, Arthur L. *Preaching and Pastoral Care.* Englewood Cliffs, N. J.: Prentice-Hall, 1964.

Thielicke, Helmut. *The Trouble with the Church.* New York: Harper & Row, 1965.

Wynn, John Charles. *Pastoral Ministry to Families.* Philadelphia: The Westminster Press, 1957.

Evangelistic Preaching

Blackwood, Andrew W. *Evangelism in the Home Church.* Nashville: Abingdon Press, 1952.

Bryan, Dawson C. *A Workable Plan of Evangelism.* Nashville: Abingdon Press, 1945.

―――. *Building Church Membership Through Evangelism.* Nashville: Abingdon Press, 1952.

Crossland, Weldon. *A Planned Program for the Church Year*. Nashville: Abingdon Press, 1951.
————. *How to Increase Church Membership and Attendance*. Nashville: Abingdon Press, 1949.
Crowe, Charles M. *The Years of Our Lord*. New York: Abingdon Press, 1955.
Dobbins, Gaines S. *Evangelism According to Christ*. Nashville: Broadman Press, 1949.
Ferris, Theodore Parker. *The Story of Jesus*. New York: Oxford University Press, 1953.
Green, Bryan. *The Practice of Evangelism*. New York: Charles Scribner's Sons, 1951.
Homrighausen, Elmer G. *Choose Ye This Day*. New York: The Westminster Press, 1943.
Hughes, Edwin Hold. *Are You an Evangelist?* Nashville: Abingdon Press, 1936.
Kennedy, Gerald. *With Singleness of Heart*. New York: Harper & Bros., 1951.
Pearce, J. Winston. *Seven First Words of Jesus*. Nashville: Broadman Press, 1966.
Sangster, W. E. *Let Me Command*. New York: Abingdon Press, 1958.
Stewart, James S. *A Faith to Proclaim*. New York: Charles Scribner's Sons, 1952.
Templeton, Charles B. *Evangelism for Tomorrow*. New York: Harper & Bros., 1957.

Preaching on the Ordinances

Baillie, Donald. *Theology of the Sacraments*. New York: Charles Scribner's Sons, 1957.
Brown, Kenneth I. *". . . and Be Baptized."* Philadelphia: Judson Press, 1952.
Brunner, Emil. *Our Faith*. New York: Charles Scribner's Sons, 1936.
Clark, John G. *Meditations on the Lord's Supper*. Nashville: Broadman Press, 1958.
Cullmann, Oscar. *Early Christian Worship*. London: SCM Press, 1952.
Fey, Harold E. *The Lord's Supper: Seven Meanings*. New York: Harper & Bros., 1948.
Forsyth, P. T. *The Church and the Sacraments*. London: Independent Press, 1949.
Foote, Gaston. *Communion Meditations*. Nashville: Abingdon Press, 1951.
Jansen, John Fredrick. *The Meaning of Baptism*. Philadelphia: The Westminster Press, 1958.
————. *Guests of God*. Philadelphia: The Westminster Press, 1956.
Jeffrey, George Johnson. *The Sacramental Table*. New York: Harper & Bros., 1954.

Kerr, Hugh Thompson. *The Christian Sacraments*. Philadelphia: The Westminster Press, 1954.

Phillips, J. B. *Appointment with God*. New York: The Macmillan Co., 1954.

Sclater, J. R. P., *The Public Worship of God*. Peterborough, N. H.: The Richard R. Smith Co., 1930.

The Midweek Service

Blair, Edward P. *The Bible and You*. New York: Abingdon Press, 1953.

Barrett and Casserley. *Dialogue on Destiny*. New York: The Seabury Press, 1955.

Deen, Edith. *All of the Women of the Bible*. New York: Harper & Bros., 1955.

Dolloff, Eugene Dinsmore. *It Can Happen Between Sundays*. Philadelphia: Judson Press, 1942.

Huss, John E. *The Hour of Power*. Grand Rapids: Zondervan Publishing House, 1955.

Lockyer, Herbert. *All the Men of the Bible*. Grand Rapids: The Zondervan Publishing House, 1958.

Mead, Frank S. *Who's Who in the Bible*. New York: Harper & Bros., 1934.

————. *What the Bible Says*. Westwood, N. J.: Fleming H. Revell Co., 1958.

Miller, Wilburn H. *Ideas for the Midweek Service*. Anderson, Ind.: Warner Press, 1956.

Nelson, Lawrence E. *Our Roving Bible*. New York: Abingdon Press, 1955.

Rolston, Holmes. *Faces About the Christ*. Richmond: John Knox Press, 1959.

————. *Personalities Around Paul*. Richmond: John Knox Press, 1954.

Pike, J. A., and Johnson, H. A. *Man in the Middle*. New York: The Seabury Press, 1956.

Smith, Roy L. *Winning Ways for Working Churches*. Nashville: Abingdon Press, 1932.

Planning Scripture Readings

Akin, J., *et al. Helping the Bible Speak*. New York: Association Press, 1956.

Ashman, Henry E. *Effective Public Reading*. Englewood Cliffs, N. J.: Prentice-Hall, 1940.

Lama, Nedra Newkirk. *How To Speak the Written Word*. Westwood, N. J.: Fleming H. Revell Co., 1949.

Lantz, J. Edward. *Reading the Bible Aloud*. New York: The Macmillan Co., 1959.

Lee, Charlotte J. *Oral Interpretation*. Boston: Houghton-Mifflin Co., 1952.

Parrish, Wayland Maxfield. *Reading Aloud*. New York: The Ronald Co., 1941.

Pierson, Arthur T. *How to Read the Word of God*. Chicago: The Moody
    Press, 1925.
Stevenson, D. E., and Diehl, C. F. *Reaching People from the Pulpit*. New
    York: Harper & Bros., 1958.
Woolbert, C. H., and Nelson, S. E. *The Art of Interpretive Speech*. New
    York: F. S. Crofts & Co., 1945.

Index